Quest

Teacher's Edition

Intro

Reading and Writing

Student Book Authors
Pamela Hartmann
Laurie Blass

Teacher's Edition Writer
Kristin Sherman

McGraw-Hill

Quest Intro Reading and Writing Teacher's Edition

Published by McGraw-Hill ESL/ELT, a business unit of The McGraw-Hill Companies, Inc., 1221 Avenue of the Americas, New York, NY 10020.

ISBN 13: 978-0-07-312834-4
ISBN 10: 0-07-312834-1
1 2 3 4 5 6 7 8 9 QPD/QPD 12 11 10 09 08 07 06

Editorial director: Erik Gundersen
Series editor: Linda O'Roke
Development editor: Christina Schafermeyer
Production manager: Juanita Thompson
Production coordinator: MaryRose Malley
Cover designer: David Averbach, Anthology
Interior designer: Karolyn Wehner

www.esl-elt.mcgraw-hill.com

The McGraw·Hill Companies

TABLE OF CONTENTS

WELCOME To The Teacher's Edition

The *Quest* Teacher's Edition provides support and flexibility to teachers using the *Quest* Student Book. Each chapter of the Teacher's Edition begins with a Chapter Overview that includes a brief summary of the Student Book chapter, a list of the vocabulary words found in the chapter, a list of the reading, critical thinking, and writing strategies highlighted throughout the chapter, as well as a list of the mechanics presented and practiced in that chapter. In addition, the Teacher's Edition provides step-by-step teaching procedures; notes on culture, grammar, vocabulary and pronunciation; expansion activities; photocopiable masters of select expansion activities; Internet research ideas; answer keys; and end-of-chapter tests.

Procedures

❍ Experienced teachers can use the step-by-step procedural notes as quick guides and refreshers before class, while newer, or substitute teachers can use the notes as a more extensive guide in the classroom. These notes also help teachers provide context for the activities and assess comprehension of the material covered.

Answer Keys

❍ Answer keys are provided for all activities that have definite answers. In cases where multiple answers could be correct, possible answers are included. Answer keys are also provided for the Vocabulary Workshop after each unit.

Notes

❍ Where appropriate, academic, culture, grammar, vocabulary and pronunciation notes provide background information, answers to questions students might raise, or points teachers might want to review or introduce. For example, in *Quest Intro Reading and Writing* Chapter 1, a reading refers to Ralph Lauren, so a cultural note provides some background information on this designer. These notes are provided at the logical point of use, but teachers can decide if and when to use the information in class.

TOEFL® iBT Tips

❍ In each chapter, six tips for the TOEFL® iBT are given with corresponding notes on how strategies and activities from the student book chapter can help students practice and prepare for the exam. Examples of TOEFL® iBT question format are also given in these tips.

Expansion Activities

❍ At least ten optional expansion activities are included in each chapter. These activities offer teachers creative ideas for reinforcing the chapter content while appealing to different learning styles. Activities include games, conversation practice, and working with manipulatives such as sentence strips, projects, and presentations. These expansion activities often allow students to practice all four language skills, not just the two skills that the student book focuses on.

Photocopiable Masters

- Up to three master worksheets that teachers can photocopy are included for each chapter. These worksheets are optional and are described in expansion activities located within the chapter. One chapter worksheet is often additional editing practice, while the others might be a graphic organizer, or a set of sentence strips.

End-of-Chapter Tests

- The end–of–chapter tests assess students on reading comprehension, one or more of the reading or critical thinking strategies highlighted in the chapter, vocabulary, mechanics and editing. Item types include multiple choice, fill-in-the-blank and true/false, for a total of 35 items per test. Answer keys are provided.

Website Research

- At the end of Part 3 in each chapter of the Teacher's Edition, you will find a list of suggested website resources that can provide additional information on the topics presented in the chapter. Teachers may use this optional resource to gather more background or to direct your students to these sites to research the topics for an expansion activity. The title of each suggested website is given and can be searched if the listed website is unavailable.

Scope and Sequenc

Chapter	Reading Strategies	Writing Strategies
UNIT 1 EDUCATION		
Chapter 1 **Identity and Learning** • Introduction: *Stories of Twins* • General Interest: *You Are the Star of Your Own Movie* • Academic: *What Makes You the Person You Are?*	• Guessing the Meanings of New Words: Dashes • Finding the Main Idea • Understanding Parts of Speech • Guessing the Meanings of New Words: Definitions	• Focus: Paragraph Describing a Childhood Influence • Strategy: Choosing a Topic
Chapter 2 **Language and Learning** • Introduction: *Emailing a Professor* • General Interest: *The Brain, Learning, and Memory* • Academic: *Methods of Learning a New Language*	• Understanding Tone • Guessing the Meanings of New Words: Examples • Using Graphic Organizers • Guessing the Meanings of New Words: Parentheses	• Focus: Paragraph Describing a Good Way to Learn a Language • Strategy: Getting Ideas
UNIT 2 BUSINESS		
Chapter 3 **Deciding on a Career** • Introduction: *Career Questionnaire* • General Interest: *Where Am I, and Where Am I Going?* • Academic: *The Joy of Work?*	• Guessing the Meanings of New Words: Commas • Understanding Pronoun References • Understanding Punctuation: Italics and Quotation Marks • Guessing the Meanings of New Words: Finding Meaning in Another Part of the Sentence or in Another Sentence	• Focus: Paragraph Describing the Perfect Career • Strategy: Writing Complete Sentences

The Mechanics of Writing	Critical Thinking Strategies
UNIT 1 EDUCATION	
• The Simple Present Tense • The Simple Past Tense • Punctuation with the Word *And* • Words in Phrases: Prepositions	• Applying Information • Comparing and Contrasting • Classifying • Estimating
• Using the Word *Or* • Punctuation with the Word *But* • Words in Phrases: Words after Prepositions • Using the Word *Because*	• Synthesizing • Recognizing Relationships Between Ideas • Applying Knowledge • Classifying
UNIT 2 BUSINESS	
• Future Tense • Possibility: *May* and *Might* • Using the Word *Or* • Using *Enjoy* and *Involve* • Adverbial Conjunctions • Words in Phrases: Words for Work	• Thinking of Solutions • Interpreting Information • Applying Information • Synthesizing

Scope and Sequence

Chapter	Reading Strategies	Writing Strategies
UNIT 2 BUSINESS		
Chapter 4 **Marketing Across Time and Space** • Introduction: *Selling Movies* • General Interest: *Advertising Through History* • Academic: *Modern Advertising*	• Guessing the Meanings of New Words: Adjective Clauses with *Who* and *That* • Making Notes • Guessing the Meanings of New Words: Colons • Finding Examples • Recognizing Word Forms	• Focus: Paragraph Describing an Advertisement • Strategy: Writing a Paragraph
UNIT 3 SOCIOLOGY		
Chapter 5 **Parenting, Gender, and Stereotypes** • Introduction: *Parenting in Chimp Society* • General Interest: *Children, Gender, and Toys* • Academic: *Stereotypes and Their Effects*	• Guessing the Meanings of New Words: *In Other Words* • Infinitives of Purpose • Understanding the Word *So* • Previewing a Reading • Guessing the Meanings of New Words: *That Is* • Finding the Main Idea: Using Topic Sentences	• Focus: Paragraph Describing an Important Lesson Learned as a Child • Strategy: Editing Your Paragraph
Chapter 6 **Becoming a Member of a Community** • Introduction: *Becoming an Adult* • General Interest: *Rites of Passage* • Academic: *Coming-of-Age Rituals*	• Guessing the Meanings of New Words: *Or* • Recognizing Key Words • Using Topic Sentences to Preview • Guessing the Meanings of New Words: Pictures and Captions • Finding Details • Understanding Words in Phrases: Verbs + Prepositions	• Focus: Paragraph Describing a Rite of Passage • Strategy: Rewriting Your Paragraph

The Mechanics of Writing	Critical Thinking Strategies
UNIT 2 BUSINESS	
The Present Continuous Tense Review: The Simple Present Tense Subject-Verb Agreement Showing Order Adjectives Adverbs Words in Phrases: *It Is, There Is/Are*	Evaluation Synthesizing
UNIT 3 SOCIOLOGY	
Using the Word *When* Using the Word *So* Review: Conjunctions Words in Phrases: *Used To* Finding Words in Phrases	Making Inferences Understanding Cause and Effect Comparing and Contrasting
Review: The Simple Present Tense Review: Subject-Verb Agreement Requirements: *Must* and *Have To* Review: Showing Order Prepositions of Place Words in Phrases: Verb + Preposition Combinations	Making Comparisons Supporting Opinions with Experiences Classifying Synthesizing

UNIT 1 EDUCATION

Unit Opener, page 1

- ❍ Direct students' attention to the photo and the unit and chapter titles on page 1. Ask questions: *What do you think the unit will be about? What do you know about this topic?*
- ❍ Brainstorm ideas for what the unit will include and write students' ideas on the board.

CHAPTER 1 IDENTITY AND LEARNING

In this chapter, students will read about different aspects of identity and personality—what makes individuals who they are. They will explore the effects of nature and nurture on personality. Nature is a person's genetic make-up. Nurture is the effect of environment and experience. Students will also think about how much they can influence what happens in their own lives. Students will read about ordinary people who are twins, and about famous people, such as the American clothing designer Ralph Lauren. The American actor John Wayne, famous for his roles in cowboy movies is mentioned as well as the American movie *Out of Africa* (1985). These topics will prepare students to write about an influence on their own lives.

VOCABULARY

adult	hero	nature	the same as	upper-class
costumes	identical	non-identical	setting	whatever
design	identity	normal	share	
determine	influence	nurture	shy	
different from	inherit	plot	similar to	
entertainment	middle-class	role	twin	

READING STRATEGIES

Guessing the Meanings of New Words: Dashes
Finding the Main Idea
Understanding Parts of Speech
Guessing the Meanings of New Words: Definitions

CRITICAL THINKING STRATEGIES

Comparing and Contrasting (Part 1)
Classifying (Part 2)
Applying Information (Part 2)
Estimating (Part 3)
Note: The strategy in bold is highlighted in the student book

MECHANICS

The Simple Present Tense
The Simple Past Tense
Punctuation with the Word *And*
Words in Phrases: Prepositions

WRITING STRATEGY

Choosing a Topic

CHAPTER 1 Identity & Learning

Chapter 1 Opener, page 3

- ❍ Direct students' attention to the photo. Ask them what they see in the photo.
- ❍ Have students discuss the four questions. This can be done in pairs, in small groups, or as a class.
- ❍ Check students' predictions of the chapter topic.

PART 1 INTRODUCTION STORIES OF TWINS, PAGES 4–6

Before Reading

Thinking Ahead

- ❍ Have students look at the photos. Ask: *Who has a brother? Who has a sister? Are you and your sister or brother identical? Which picture shows two people who are identical? What does identical mean?*
- ❍ Have students read the questions in the book.
- ❍ Put students in pairs to discuss and answer the questions.
- ❍ Call on students to share their answers with the class.

ANSWER KEY

Answers will vary.

EXPANSION ACTIVITY: Find Someone Who

- ❍ Photocopy the Black Line Master *Find Someone Who* on page BLM 1 and distribute to students.
- ❍ Model the activity. Call on a student and ask: *Do you have two or more sisters?* Continue asking until someone answers *yes*. Point out that when you find someone who answers *yes*, you can then write that person's name on the first line.
- ❍ Have students stand and walk around the room asking questions until they can write someone's name next to each item. Point out that they can only use a classmate's name once. Tell students there may be some questions no one answers *yes* to. For such questions students should write *no one* on the line.
- ❍ When students have completed the worksheet, call on students to tell the class something they learned *(Lee has more than two sisters.)*. Ask if there were any questions no one answered *yes* to.

Reading

- ❍ Have students look at the reading. Ask: *What is this story about?* (*twins*). Go over the directions and the question.
- ❍ Have students read the passage silently, or have students follow along silently as you play the audio program.
- ❍ Ask students what they found surprising about the sets of twins.

EXPANSION ACTIVITY: Same and Different

- ❍ Put students in pairs. Have them work together to list things that are the same and things that are different about Mark and Gerald from the reading.
- ❍ Tell students that the characteristics must be things that cannot be seen (*height* should not be listed, but *likes Chinese food* can be listed).
- ❍ Call on students to share their ideas with the class.
- ❍ Set a time limit of one minute.

ANSWER KEY

Same: like John Wayne movies, like wrestling, work as firefighters

Different: grew up in different families, in different towns, went to different schools, had different friends

After Reading

A. Check Your Understanding

- ❍ Go over the directions.
- ❍ Have students fill in *T* or *F* next to each sentence.
- ❍ Have students check their answers with a partner.
- ❍ Go over the answers with the class. For additional practice, have students correct the false statements.

ANSWER KEY

1. T; 2. F; 3. T; 4. T; 5. F; 6. F; 7. T

Corrected False Statements:

2. They did not grow up in the same home. OR They grew up in different homes.
5. As children, Jim Springer and Jim Lewis didn't live together.
6. They liked the same things.

B. Talk About It

❍ Go over the directions and the examples.

❍ Model the activity with a student. Ask: *Is your appearance the same as your brother's or sister's?* Point out where you would put a check mark in the chart.

❍ Put students in pairs to ask and answer the questions to complete the chart.

❍ Call on students to tell the class something about their partners' answers *(Maria's likes and dislikes are different from her sister's.)*. Remind students to use the expressions *the same as, similar to,* and *different from* in their answers.

ANSWER KEY

Answers will vary.

CRITICAL THINKING STRATEGY: Comparing and Contrasting

❍ Explain to students that comparing and contrasting are ways to analyze what we know about a topic, and can help us understand a topic better.

❍ Point out that Activity B and the following Venn diagram expansion activity allow students to compare and contrast themselves with another person.

EXPANSION ACTIVITY: Venn Diagrams

❍ Photocopy the Black Line Master *Family Characteristics* on page BLM 2 and distribute to students.

❍ Draw a Venn diagram like the one below on the board. Write *me* above the circle on the left and *my sister* (or brother/other relative) above the circle on the right.

❍ Model the activity. Tell something about yourself that is different from your brother or sister and write it on the diagram in the appropriate place. Tell something that is the same as your brother or sister and write it in the overlapping section of the diagram.

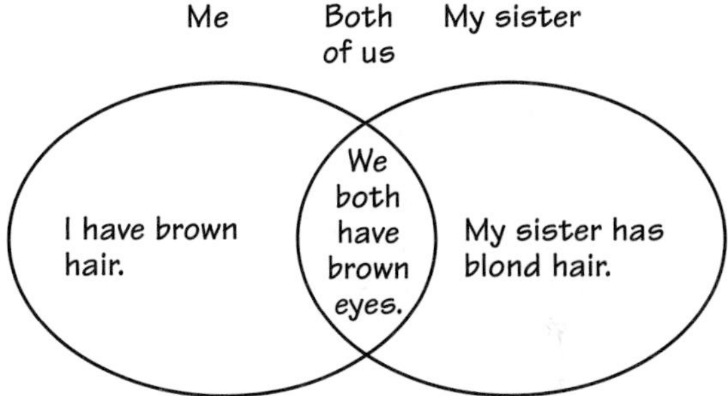

❍ Have your students complete the Venn diagrams to illustrate things that are the same for them and a brother or sister or other relative, and things that are different for them.

❍ Put students in pairs to explain their Venn diagrams to each other.

❍ Ask for volunteers to share their Venn diagram with the class.

PART 2 GENERAL INTEREST READING

YOU ARE THE STAR OF YOUR OWN MOVIE, PAGES 7–13

Before Reading

A. Making Predictions

❍ Direct students' attention to the photos on page 7. Ask students what it means to make predictions (*make a guess about future actions*). Point out that we can use visuals such as photos, graphs, and cartoons to make predictions about content.

❍ Have students think about what the reading will be about and discuss ideas with a partner.

B. Vocabulary Preparation

- ❍ Go over the directions. Have students look at the definitions. Explain unfamiliar terms if necessary.
- ❍ If your students need more help with pronunciation, read the definitions aloud and have students repeat, then read the sentences aloud and have students repeat.
- ❍ Have students match the rest of the definitions to the words in blue by writing the letters on the lines next to the sentences.
- ❍ Have students check their answers with a partner.
- ❍ Go over the answers with the class.

ANSWER KEY

1. e; 2. c; 3. a; 4. f; 5. d; 6. g; 7. b

EXPANSION ACTIVITY: Beanbag Toss

- ❍ Tell students they have one minute to review the vocabulary from Activity B.
- ❍ After one minute, ask students to close their books.
- ❍ Tell students that you will call on a student and toss a ball or beanbag. You will say one of the definitions, and the student should respond with the vocabulary word and throw the ball or beanbag back.
- ❍ Call on a student and toss the ball or beanbag, saying *star*. Elicit *hero* from the student.
- ❍ Repeat with other students. This should be a fast-paced activity.

READING STRATEGY: Guessing the Meanings of New Words: Dashes

- ❍ Go over the information in the box. Ask: *What is a dash? What does* context *mean?*
- ❍ Point out that sometimes dashes come in pairs. In that case, the definition or explanation is between the two dashes.

C. Guessing the Meanings of New Words: Dashes

- ❍ Go over the directions.
- ❍ Have students look over the reading. Elicit examples of information that follow dashes in the text.

TOEFL® iBT Tip

TOEFL iBT TIP 1: The TOEFL iBT tests the ability to determine the meanings of words in context.

- ❍ Point out that the strategy and activity *Guessing the Meanings of New Words: Dashes*, will help students improve their vocabulary for the TOEFL iBT. By identifying words that are in *apposition to* (next to) other words and understanding their meanings, students will be able to apply this information toward further understanding the concepts presented in the text.

On the TOEFL iBT this question appears in the following format:

The word________ in the passage is closest in meaning to…

Reading

- ❍ Go over the directions and the question.
- ❍ Have students read the passage silently, or have students follow along as you play the audio program.
- ❍ Ask students how Ralph Lauren's life is like a movie.

Culture Note:

- ❍ Ralph Lauren is a well-known American fashion designer. He created the Polo clothing line. His ads can be found in magazines and on television. They feature beautiful, rich people often in outdoor settings.

EXPANSION ACTIVITY: Ask and Answer

- Have students work individually to write words and definitions that are indicated by dashes in the text *(middle-class, movie, identity, shy, roles, costumes, scenes, actors, plot).*
- Model the activity. Call on a student and ask: *What is a costume?* Elicit that it is the clothing worn in a movie or play.
- Put students in pairs to take turns asking and answering questions about the words in the reading.
- Call on students to tell the class what they think each word means.

After Reading

READING STRATEGY: Finding the Main Idea

- Go over the information in the box. Ask: *What is a main idea? Where can you sometimes find the main idea?*

A. Main Idea

- Go over the directions. Have students fill in the bubble next to the main idea. Encourage them to review the reading if necessary.
- Go over the answer with the class.

ANSWER KEY

C

TOEFL® iBT Tip

TOEFL iBT TIP 2: The TOEFL iBT does not directly test the ability to determine the main idea in a text. Instead, examinees are required to recognize the minor, less important ideas that do not belong in a summary; or, they may be required to distinguish between major and minor points of information.

- Point out that the strategy for *Finding the Main Idea* will help students distinguish between major and minor points in a text on the TOEFL iBT.

- Explain to students that this type of question is called a *prose summary* or *classification* question, and partial credit will be given for correct answers. On the TOEFL iBT, the answers to this type of question are not in traditional multiple-choice format.

- Students will also benefit from doing Activity D, *Application,* on student book pages 12–13, to prepare for the classification or summary question type.

The classification or summary question type appears in the form of a schematic table that requires examinees to select and drag answer choices to specific positions in a chart.

B. Vocabulary Check

- Direct students' attention to the words in the box. Say each word and have students repeat.
- Go over the directions and the example.
- Have students fill in the blanks and then check their answers with a partner.
- Go over the answers with the class.

ANSWER KEY

1. shy; 2. middle-class; 3. role; 4. identity; 5. costumes; 6. plot; 7. setting

READING STRATEGY: Understanding Parts of Speech

❍ Go over the information in the box.
Ask comprehension questions such as: *What is an example of a noun? An adjective? A verb? What does an adjective do? What part of speech is* identity?

❍ Write two sentences on the board *(My younger sister looks like me. Henry's brother works at a big store.)*. Have the students identify different parts of speech in the sentences.

TOEFL® iBT Tip

TOEFL iBT TIP 3: The TOEFL iBT measures the ability to understand specific words and phrases selected by the author and used in the passage.

❍ Point out that the strategy *Understanding Parts of Speech,* and the following activity, *Working with Words*, will help students improve their vocabulary for the TOEFL iBT.

❍ Useful vocabulary words or phrases from the reading include the following: *middle-class, be whatever you want to be, pronounce, hero, learn to hide,* and *plot.*

On the TOEFL iBT this question may appear in the following format:

In stating ________, the author means that . . .

C. Working with Words

❍ Go over the directions.

❍ Have students identify the parts of speech for each word they wrote on the lines in Activity B.

❍ Go over the answers.

ANSWER KEY

1. adj; 2. adj; 3. n; 4. n; 5. n; 6. n; 7. n

CRITICAL THINKING STRATEGY: Classifying

❍ Explain that when we classify, we organize information into groups, classes, or categories. This can help students remember information better.

❍ Point out that the reading strategy of understanding parts of speech is also a type of classification. Activity C, *Working with Words*, and the following expansion activity, *More Practice*, use this critical thinking strategy.

EXPANSION ACTIVITY: More Practice

❍ For a greater challenge, have students identify all the nouns, verbs, and adjectives in the sentences in Activity B (on student book page 10). Put a chart like the following on the board:

NOUNS	VERBS	ADJECTIVES

❍ Have students complete the chart with words from the sentences in Activity B and then compare answers with a partner. Note that students do not need to classify the words they wrote on the lines again.

❍ Go over the answers with the class.

ANSWER KEY

NOUNS		VERBS	ADJECTIVES
Jenny	Neal Gabler	was	afraid
people	part	thinks	small
Peter	dresses	comes	rich
family	suits	is	poor
town	man	were	old
John Wayne	Miami	played	beautiful
cowboy	firefighter	goes	long
movies	Hawaii	give	fine
ideas		tries	young

CRITICAL THINKING STRATEGY: Applying Information

- Go over the information in the box. Elicit other words for *apply* (e.g., *use*). Ask: *What questions can you ask to apply information?*

D. Application

- Go over the directions.
- Have students look at the example. Ask questions such as: *Who is this "movie" about? What does she usually wear? Where has she lived? What happens in this "movie"?*
- Have students complete the chart on the following page with information about themselves.

ANSWER KEY

Answers will vary.

E. Discussion

- Put students in small groups to talk about their "movies."
- Call on students to tell the class about their lives as movies.

EXPANSION ACTIVITY: Picture It!

- Have students bring in magazines, or bring in magazines yourself. Distribute scissors, glue or tape, and paper.
- Tell students to make a collage about their lives using pictures from the magazines.
- Put students in small groups to share magazines. Have them tear out pictures and make collages to illustrate their lives and/or future.
- When the collages are complete, have students talk with their small groups about their lives as shown in their collages.
- Display the collages in the classroom. You can give students time to walk around to look at the collages and discuss.

PART 3 ACADEMIC READING WHAT MAKES YOU THE PERSON YOU ARE?, PAGES 14–18

Before Reading

A. Making Predictions

- Direct students' attention to the photo. Ask: *Who do you see? What do you think is their relationship? Who is the oldest? The youngest?*
- Go over the directions. Explain any unfamiliar terms *(personality, independent, dependent, characteristics, serious).*
- Have students look at the words in the box. Read each characteristic aloud and have students repeat.
- Have students write the appropriate characteristics under each position in the family and then compare their ideas with a partner.
- Call on students to share their ideas with the class. Point out that they might have different ideas.
- Explain that by anticipating the content of the reading in this activity, they are more likely to understand and remember it.

ANSWER KEY

Answers will vary.

EXPANSION ACTIVITY: Characteristic Line-Up

- Have a group of students stand at the front of the room. Tell students that you will call out a characteristic and they should rate themselves on a scale of 1 to 10, with 10 meaning that they have that characteristic to a very high degree and 1 meaning not at all. Indicate by pointing that one side of the room is 1 and the other side is 10.
- Call out one of the characteristics *(a leader)* and have students move. Tell them they can stand anywhere on the continuum from 1 to 10 that indicates how much they think they have that characteristic compared to people in their family.
- Call on students at either end of the continuum

and ask them about their positions in their own families.
- Repeat with other characteristics and different groups of students.

B. Thinking Ahead

- Go over the directions.
- Have students look at the chart. Point out that they are just making an estimate about percentages—they don't have to actually know the percentages.
- Have students complete the chart and then compare their ideas with a partner.
- Call on students to tell the class about their ideas.

ANSWER KEY

Answers will vary.

CRITICAL THINKING STRATEGY: Estimating

- Explain that when we estimate, we are using what we know to make guesses about the unknown.
- Point out that we estimate all the time in our daily lives. Elicit examples from students about things they estimate *(the cost of meals, the time it takes to do a task).*

C. Vocabulary Preparation

- Go over the directions.
- Have students match the definitions to the words and then check their answers with a partner.
- Go over the answers with the class.

ANSWER KEY

1. b; 2. a; 3. c

EXPANSION ACTIVITY: Pair Share

- Have students work individually to brainstorm a list of things they inherited from their parents.
- Put students in pairs to share their lists.
- Call on students to tell the class about one thing their partner inherited.

READING STRATEGY: Guessing the Meanings of New Words: Definitions

- Go over the information in the box.
- For extra practice, have students write definitions for words from the unit using *is, are,* or *means.*

D. Practice: Guessing the Meanings of New Words: Definitions

- Go over the directions.
- Have students skim the passage for the word *nurture* and its definition.

Reading

- Go over the directions and the question.
- Have students read the passage silently, or play the audio program and have students follow along silently.

Pronunciation Note:

- You may want to point out how numbers are pronounced. You could play the audio program again and have students listen for the pronunciation of numbers.

After Reading

A. Main Idea

- Review what a main idea is and elicit where it can sometimes be found.
- Read the questions aloud.
- Have students write answers to the questions and then check their answers with a partner.
- Go over the answers with the class.

ANSWER KEY

1. was; 2. followed; 3. did; 4. did; 5. joined; 6. played; 7. wore; 8. wanted; 9. read; 10. tried; 11. bothered; 12. didn't get; 13. went; 14. gave; 15. is/was

TOEFL® iBT Tip

TOEFL iBT TIP 5: Although the TOEFL iBT does not discretely test grammar skills, examinees' essay scores will be determined based on the range of grammar and vocabulary used in their essays.

❍ Point out that the grammar activities in *The Mechanics of Writing* part of this chapter will help them improve their use of verb tenses for essay writing.

Punctuation with the Word *And*

❍ Go over the information in the box. Ask: *When should we use a comma with* and*?*

D. Practice: Punctuation with the Word *And*

❍ Go over the directions.
❍ Have students combine the sentences using *and*.
❍ Have students pay attention to when the verb needs to change.
❍ Have students check their answers with a partner.
❍ Go over the answers with the class.

Grammar Notes:

❍ Some students may not be familiar with what words can be deleted when sentences are combined. You may want to point out that words that are repeated in each section being combined can be dropped.
❍ You can use these examples to illustrate the point:

I like apples. I like bananas. I like apples and ~~I like~~ bananas.

We work at the same place. We go to the same school. We work at the same place and ~~we~~ go to the same school.

ANSWER KEY

1. I like baseball and wrestling.
2. Nature and nurture are important.
3. Ralph designed jeans, boots, and suits.
4. Education, family, and culture are part of nurture.
5. My brother played tennis, and my sister played soccer.
6. I went to the movie and liked it a lot.
7. Mary and Kim are the same height and weight, and they have the same hair color. *OR* Mary and Kim have the same height, weight, and hair color.
8. Mike and John grew up in different towns and went to different schools.
9. Jessie is shy, musical, and intelligent.
10. One sister is a teacher, and the other sister is a designer.

TOEFL® iBT Tip

TOEFL iBT TIP 6: Both the integrated and independent essays of the TOEFL iBT will be scored based on how well the examinee completes the overall writing task. However, the writing section also requires that the essay follow the conventions of spelling, punctuation, and layout.

❍ Point out that the punctuation activities in *The Mechanics of Writing* part of this chapter will help students improve their coherence and the flow of ideas in their essays.

Words in Phrases: Prepositions

❍ Go over the information in the box.
❍ Ask: *What are examples of prepositions? What common phrases include prepositions? Why should we learn these phrases?*

Vocabulary Note:

❍ You may want to point out that it is easier to remember and use new vocabulary when we learn it as part of a phrase. This helps non-native speakers become more fluent.

E. Practice: Finding Words in Phrases

- Go over the directions.
- Have students underline and circle the correct words in the remaining sentences and identify the parts of speech. Have students note that there may be more than one preposition in a sentence.
- Have students check their answers with a partner.
- Go over the answers with the class.

ANSWER KEY

1. influence (on) (noun)
2. interested (in) (adjective)
3. different (from) (adjective)
4. similar (to) (adjective)
5. hero (of) (noun)
6. form (of) (noun)
7. combination (of) (noun)
8. afraid (of) (adjective)
9. stories (about) (noun)
10. talked (about) (verb); importance (of) (noun)

EXPANSION ACTIVITY: Sentence Chain

- Model the activity: Call on a student and say a phrase *(similar to)*. Elicit an original sentence from the student using that phrase.
- Have that student call on a classmate and say a phrase from Activity E. The classmate should make an original sentence using that phrase.
- Continue the activity until all the phrases from Activity E have been used.

F. Review: Editing a Paragraph

- Go over the directions.
- Have students find and correct the seven mistakes. Have them check their answers with a partner.
- Go over the answers with the class.

ANSWER KEY

The actress Audrey Hepburn was an influence ~~of~~ ^on me as a child. I loved her old movies. She seemed very different ~~of~~ ^from people in my life. She was beautiful / and elegant. She ~~have~~ ^had a wonderful accent. After I ~~see~~ ^saw her in one movie, I wanted my hair and clothes to be similar ^to hers. She was a lovely lady ^, and I wanted to be like her.

PART 5 ACADEMIC WRITING, PAGES 24–27

Writing Assignment

- Go over the directions and the question.

Model

- Have students read the six steps of the example.
- Direct students' attention to Step A of the example, and ask: *What topic did the student choose?*
- Direct students' attention to Step B. Ask: *What questions did the student use to get ideas?* Elicit other ways to gather ideas.
- Direct students' attention to Step C. Elicit examples of the information the student included, and why the information is helpful. Point out that specific examples (e.g., *She went to Egypt and rode a camel.*) are more interesting than general ideas (e.g., *She traveled and did fun things.*). Ask students if they notice any mistakes.
- Have students read the paragraph in Step D of the example. Ask questions such as: *Does the paragraph start out in a general way or with specific details? When does the writer mention the topic of the paragraph first? How does the writer end the paragraph? How is it different from the sentences in Step C?*
- Direct students' attention to Step E. Ask: *How many mistakes did the writer circle in the paragraph in Step D? What are they?*
- Have students read the paragraph in Step F. Ask: *How did the writer correct the mistakes?*

Your Turn

❍ Go over the directions and questions.

WRITING STRATEGY: Choosing a Topic

❍ Go over the information in the box. Ask: *What two things should help you choose your topic?*

(Your Turn, *continued*)

❍ Have students read Step A and choose a topic.

❍ Have students answer the questions in Step B. You may want to put students in pairs to discuss their ideas.

❍ Have students complete Steps C and D. Remind students not to worry about mistakes yet. If you want to have your students practice peer editing skills, have them exchange paragraphs with a partner and comment on mistakes or other problems.

❍ Ask students to edit their paragraphs (Step E) and then rewrite (Step F).

❍ Collect the paragraphs.

EXPANSION ACTIVITY: Who Is It?

❍ After you collect the paragraphs, redistribute them so each student has another student's paragraph.

❍ Call on students to read the paragraphs aloud. Have the other students in the class guess who wrote the paragraph.

UNIT 1 EDUCATION

CHAPTER 2 LANGUAGE LEARNING

In this chapter, students will read about the brain, learning, and memory. They will explore the effects of a "rich environment" on the brain. They will find out what helps us to remember. In addition, students will read about five different methods of language learning. The readings in this chapter should help students become more aware of how they are learning English and how they can better remember what they learn. One reading is a review of a book by Eric Jensen, *Teaching with the Brain in Mind*. Jensen is an American educator and trainer who has taught at elementary school through university levels and currently provides training on learning and the brain.

VOCABULARY

academic material	commands	the Natural Approach	problem-solving exercise
active	the content-based approach	neurons	respond
approach	focus on	note-taking	solution
bilingual dictionary	the grammar-translation method	passage	stimulation
bits	the lexical approach	phrases	strategies
challenging	memorize	physical action	target language
chunks	mnemonic	physically	Total Physical Response (TPR)

READING STRATEGIES

Understanding Tone
Guessing the Meanings of New Words: Examples
Using Graphic Organizers
Guessing the Meanings of New Words: Parentheses

CRITICAL THINKING STRATEGIES

Classifying (Part 2)
Recognizing Relationships Between Ideas (Part 2)
Applying Knowledge (Part 2)
Synthesizing (Part 3)
Note: The strategy in bold is highlighted in the student book.

MECHANICS

Using the Word *Or*
Punctuation with the Word *But*
Words in Phrases: Words after Prepositions
Using the Word *Because*

WRITING STRATEGY

Getting Ideas

CHAPTER 2 Language Learning

Chapter 2 Opener, page 29

- ❍ Direct students' attention to the photo. Ask them what is happening in the photo.
- ❍ Have students discuss the four questions. This can be done in pairs, in small groups, or as a class.
- ❍ Check students' predictions of the chapter topic.

PART 1 INTRODUCTION
EMAILING A PROFESSOR, PAGES 30–33

Before Reading

Thinking Ahead

- ❍ Have students look at the photo at the top of page 30. Ask: *Who is in the photo? What are they doing? How do you think they feel?*
- ❍ Have students read the questions and write brief answers.
- ❍ Put students in pairs to share their ideas.
- ❍ Call on students to share their answers with the class.

ANSWER KEY

1. Answers may vary but might include the following: the student will miss material, will not know what is going on in class.
2. Answers may vary but should mention the following: the student should talk to the teacher or other students to find out what he or she missed.
3. *(reading from left to right)* b, d, a, c

EXPANSION ACTIVITY: Make Predictions

- ❍ Put students in pairs.
- ❍ Have students read the sample exam questions from Question 3 in the *Thinking Ahead* activity.
- ❍ Ask students to brainstorm a list of topics that might be addressed in this chapter based on the sample questions.
- ❍ Call on students to share their ideas with the class.

Reading

- ❍ Go over the directions and the question.
- ❍ Have students read the emails silently, or have students follow along silently as you play the audio program.
- ❍ Ask students what problem Maria and Jennifer have *(They both were absent from class and there is an exam on Friday.)*.

EXPANSION ACTIVITY: Stop and Think

- ❍ Tell students that they can learn more from a reading if they make connections between the reading and their own experiences or previous knowledge.
- ❍ For each email in the reading, ask students to write notes about what the email reminded them of. Ask questions to serve as prompts: *Did you ever receive or send an email like this one? Have you been in this situation before? What is the relationship between the people in each email?* Set a time limit of one minute.
- ❍ When students have finished writing their notes, put students in pairs to share their ideas.
- ❍ Call on students to share their ideas with the class.

After Reading

A. Check Your Understanding

- ❍ Go over the directions.
- ❍ Have students fill in *T* or *F* next to each sentence.
- ❍ Have students check their answers with a partner.
- ❍ Go over the answers with the class. For additional practice, have students correct the false statements.

ANSWER KEY

1. T; 2. F; 3. F; 4. T; 5. T

Corrected False Statements:

2. There is going to be an exam on Friday.
3. The class is in education.

EXPANSION ACTIVITY: Partner Challenge

- Have students write five more true/false statements about the information in the emails.
- Put students in pairs to take turns reading the statements to their partners. Partners should say if the statement is true or false. Walk around the room to monitor the activity and provide help as needed.
- Call on students to read statements to the class. Elicit from the class if the statements are true or false.

READING STRATEGY: Understanding Tone

- Go over the information in the box.
- Ask: *When do we use an informal tone? A formal tone? What are some differences between the two? With which tone are we really careful about spelling? With which tone do we use multiple punctuation marks?*

B. Talk About It

- Go over the directions.
- Put students in pairs to answer the questions.
- Call on students to share their ideas with the class.

Culture Notes:

- The widespread use of the Internet and email has created changes in the way people write and the language they use. Users have also developed certain rules of courtesy regarding emails.
- In emails, users show emotion through the use of symbols or combinations of punctuation marks (☺). These are called *emoticons.*
- The special rules of courtesy users observe in emails is called *netiquette.* The following expansion activity helps students explore these rules.

ANSWER KEY

1. Email 2 is the most formal because Maria is writing to the teacher, who is above her social position.
2. Email 1 is the most informal because Maria is writing to a friend.
3. One can tell the email is informal because it is used with a friend, with someone of the same social position. Characteristics of informal style found are the use of incorrect spelling (*gonna*) and slang (*stuff*), the display of emotion, and the use of multiple punctuation marks.

EXPANSION ACTIVITY: Online Research

- Point out that people who write emails should follow certain rules of etiquette, or politeness, especially when at school or work.
- Brainstorm a list of rules that students usually follow when writing emails.
- For an out-of-class or lab assignment, have students use a search engine and enter the word "netiquette."
- Ask students to write down three rules of netiquette that they find in their research.
- Call on students to share their ideas with the class.

PART  GENERAL INTEREST READING THE BRAIN, LEARNING, AND MEMORY, PAGES 33–37

Before Reading

A. Thinking Ahead

- Go over the directions.
- Direct students' attention to the picture and ask: *What is the picture of? What do you know about the brain and learning?*
- Put students in pairs or small groups to answer the questions.
- Call on students to share their ideas with the class.

ANSWER KEY

Answers will vary.

B. Vocabulary Preparation

- ❍ Go over the directions.
- ❍ Have students read the first sentence. Ask students how they can tell the meaning of the word in blue (*set off by dashes*).
- ❍ Have students circle the meaning of the word in blue in each sentence.
- ❍ Have students check their answers with a partner.
- ❍ Go over the answers with the class.

ANSWER KEY

1. method; 2. brain cells; 3. something new to experience; 4. difficult, but not too difficult; 5. an answer to the problem; 6. technique to help the memory

EXPANSION ACTIVITY: Beanbag Toss

- ❍ Tell students they have one minute to review the vocabulary from Activity B.
- ❍ After one minute, ask students to close their books.
- ❍ Call on a student and toss a ball or a beanbag while you say a definition (*brain cells*). Elicit the vocabulary word (*neurons*) from the student as he or she tosses the ball or beanbag back.
- ❍ Continue the activity until students have practiced all the new words.

READING STRATEGY: Guessing the Meanings of New Words: Examples

- ❍ Go over the information in the box. Ask: *What are some words that come before examples?*

C. Guessing the Meanings of New Words: Examples

- ❍ Go over the directions.
- ❍ Have students skim the reading. Elicit examples of phrases they find that introduce examples.
- ❍ Remind students to pay attention to these phrases as they read.

TOEFL® iBT Tip

TOEFL iBT TIP 1: The TOEFL iBT tests the ability to determine the meaning of words in context.

- ❍ Point out that the previous activity, *Guessing the Meanings of New Words,* will help students improve their vocabulary for the TOEFL iBT. By identifying words that are defined, students will be able to apply this information toward further understanding the concepts presented in the rest of the passage.

- ❍ Useful vocabulary words or phrases from the reading include the following: *neurons, linguistic memory,* and *mnemonics*

On the TOEFL iBT this question appears in the following format:

The word ________ in the passage is closest in meaning to ...

Reading

- ❍ Go over the directions and the question.
- ❍ Have students read the passage silently, or follow along silently as you play the audio program.
- ❍ Ask: *How can we learn and remember things well?* Elicit answers and write them on the board.

CRITICAL THINKING STRATEGY: Classifying

- ❍ Point out that classifying, or putting things in groups, is an important critical thinking strategy. It allows us to notice what things have in common, and to make connections between the ideas.
- ❍ The following expansion activity gives students an opportunity to use classifying skills to review the passage.

EXPANSION ACTIVITY: Reconstruction

❍ Photocopy the Black Line Master *Reconstruction* on page BLM 3. Students will work in pairs, so copy enough for each pair of students.
❍ Cut the worksheet along the dotted lines and put each set in an envelope or ziplock bag.
❍ Have students form pairs and distribute a set of strips to each pair of students.
❍ Have students reconstruct the reading outline by putting the details and headings in order.
❍ Ask volunteers to recreate the outline on the board.

ANSWER KEY

Part 1: Introduction
- Teaching methods change over time.
- Eric Jensen wrote *Teaching with the Brain in Mind* about the brain and learning.

Part 2: Learning and the Brain
- Genes determine 30–60 percent of brain connections.
- Education and life experience determine 40–70 percent of brain connections.
- The brain cells of both children and adults grow new connections in a rich environment.

Part 3: What is a "Rich" Environment?
- Stimulation is the main characteristic of a rich environment.
- Stimulation is challenging.
- Problem-solving (puzzles, discussions, word games) stimulates the brain.
- Neurons grow when the brain works.

Part 4: The Brain and Memory
- There are different types of memory, including linguistic memory and body learning.
- We remember best in chunks, or groups of words.
- Mnemonics are a good way to remember chunks.
- Body memory, such as riding a bike, lasts a long time.
- The brain and body remember together.

Part 5: Conclusion
- This book is good for students and teachers.

After Reading

A. Main Idea

❍ Go over the directions. Have students fill in the correct bubble for the main idea. Encourage them to review the reading if necessary.
❍ Go over the answer with the class.

ANSWER KEY

B

READING STRATEGY: Using Graphic Organizers

❍ Go over the information in the box.

Academic Note:

❍ Different types of organizers may be more useful than others for presenting some types of information. If your students are familiar with graphic organizers, elicit examples and write them on the board. If not, you may want to present the following graphic organizers:
- Venn diagram (from Chapter 1, Black Line Master *Family Characteristics*): for comparing and contrasting two things.
- T-chart: for comparing two things, or classifying.

B. Finding Details

❍ Go over the directions.
❍ Have students complete the tree diagrams and then compare their ideas with a partner.
❍ Go over the answers with the class.
❍ Ask students what relationships between ideas are represented by the two organizers (*1 = cause and effect, 2 = classification*).

ANSWER KEY

1. Connections in the brain: genes, education/life experience; 2. Two kinds of memory: linguistic memory, body learning

TOEFL® iBT Tip

TOEFL iBT TIP 2: The TOEFL iBT tests the ability to understand key facts and important information contained within a text. Locating key words in a text will help students build vocabulary and improve their reading skills.

- Point out that the reading section of the TOEFL iBT may require examinees to identify information that is NOT included in the passage.
- The activity *Finding Details* requires students to connect information in a graphic organizer. This will help to scaffold students' abilities upward toward mastering the schematic table questions on the test.
- Students will also benefit from doing Activity C, *Vocabulary Check* in order to prepare for the classification or summary question type.

The question type appears in the form of a schematic table that requires examinees to select and drag answer choices to specific positions in a chart.

CRITICAL THINKING STRATEGY: Recognizing Relationships Between Ideas

- Point out to students that an important critical thinking strategy is the ability to recognize the relationships between ideas. Suggest that they pay attention to words that signal relationships.

EXPANSION ACTIVITY: Signal Words

- Some verbs that indicate cause and effect relationships are: *cause, affect,* and *determine*. Other words include: *because, due to, since,* and *consequently.*
- Brainstorm with students a list of words that may indicate classification (*type, class, kind*).

C. Vocabulary Check

- Go over the directions.
- Have students fill in the chart with examples from the reading.
- Go over the answers.

ANSWER KEY

Word or Phrase	Examples
problem-solving exercises	word games, puzzles, discussions, real problems
chunks	group of words, a sentence, or a song
bits	one letter, one word, one note of music
physical actions	sports, dance, moving around the classroom

EXPANSION ACTIVITY: Create a Mnemonic

- Brainstorm a list of ideas from the reading that could be remembered in chunks (e.g., *examples of problem-solving activities, types of linguistic memory).*
- Put students in pairs to create a mnemonic to remember information from the reading.
- Call on students to share their mnemonic devices with the class.

CRITICAL THINKING STRATEGY:
Applying Knowledge

- ❍ Using what you already know in new situations is an important critical thinking strategy. This strategy helps you remember new information.

D. Application

- ❍ Go over the directions.
- ❍ Put students in small groups to answer the questions.
- ❍ Call on students to share their ideas with the class.

ANSWER KEY

Answers will vary.

EXPANSION ACTIVITY: Memory Chain Game

- ❍ Tell students that they will learn something about their classmates in this activity.
- ❍ Model the activity. Tell the class something you enjoy doing (*My name is _______ and I like swimming*). As you speak, act out swimming. Call on a student to introduce you to the class and act out your movement. Then the student should say his or her name and something he or she enjoys, while acting out the activity.
- ❍ If you have a large class, divide the class into smaller groups of 10 or 12 students.
- ❍ Have the students form a circle. One student will begin, saying his or her name and activity and demonstrating the activity. The next student will repeat the first student's information and action, and add his or her own. The next student will repeat the information and actions for the previous students. Each group should continue in this way until the circle is complete. Other students may help prompt if a student forgets someone's action.
- ❍ Call on students to share their thoughts about the activity and body memory. Ask students how many people's activities they can remember.

PART 3 ACADEMIC READING
METHODS OF LEARNING A NEW LANGUAGE, PAGES 38–43

Before Reading

A. Thinking Ahead

- ❍ Direct students' attention to the illustrations. Ask: *Who do you see? What are they doing? Which one looks the most fun? Which activity do you prefer?*
- ❍ Go over the directions.
- ❍ Put students in small groups to answer the questions.
- ❍ Call on students to share their ideas with the class.

ANSWER KEY

Answers will vary.

EXPANSION ACTIVITY: Preference Line-Up

- ❍ Have a group of students come to the front of the room.
- ❍ Tell these students that they will form a continuum to reflect their preferences in language learning. Explain that you will say a type of activity and identify one side of the room as *don't like it at all,* and the other side as *like it very much.*
- ❍ Say a type of activity (*pair discussion*) and have students move. Call on a couple of students to explain their position.
- ❍ Continue with one or two other activities (*listening to a lecture, puzzles*).
- ❍ Call another group of students to the board and repeat with other language learning activities (*listening to audiotapes, playing games*).
- ❍ Ask questions about the activity: *Do all students like the same thing? What activities seem most popular? Which ones have you had the most experience with?*

B. Vocabulary Preparation

❍ Go over the directions.
❍ Have students match the definitions to the words and then check their answers with a partner.
❍ Go over the answers with the class.

ANSWER KEY

1. d; 2. f; 3. e; 4. c; 5. b; 6. a

READING STRATEGY: Guessing the Meanings of New Words: Parentheses

❍ Go over the information in the box.
❍ Point out or elicit that parentheses are similar to dashes—both are types of punctuation that can signal a definition or explanation.

C. Guessing the Meanings of New Words: Parentheses

❍ Go over the directions.

TOEFL® iBT Tip

TOEFL iBT TIP 3: The TOEFL iBT measures the ability to understand specific words and phrases selected by the author and used in the passage.

❍ Point out that the strategy and activity for *Guessing the Meanings of New Words: Parentheses* will help students improve their vocabulary for the TOEFL iBT. By understanding words expressed in parentheses, students will be able to apply this information toward understanding the passage.

❍ Useful vocabulary words or phrases from the reading include the following: *target language, phrases,* and *groups of words.*

On the TOEFL iBT this question may appear in the following format:

In stating ________ *the author means that . . .*

Reading

❍ Go over the directions and the question.
❍ Direct students' attention to the beginning of the reading and ask: *What is this? Who is the writer? Why is she writing this?* Students should notice that this is the essay exam for the class discussed in the earlier emails from the reading in Part 1.
❍ Have students read the essay exam silently or follow along as you play the audio program.
❍ When students have finished, elicit the five methods for teaching or learning a new language (*grammar translation, TPR, the lexical approach, the Natural Approach, content-based approach*).

After Reading

A. Check Your Understanding

❍ Go over the directions.
❍ Have students match the methods and main points and then check their answers with a partner.
❍ Go over the answers with the class.

ANSWER KEY

1. c; 2. d; 3. e; 4. a; 5. b

B. Vocabulary Check

❍ Go over the directions.
❍ Have students complete the chart with the meanings of the words or terms and then compare charts with a partner.
❍ Go over the answers with the class.

ANSWER KEY

Word or Term	Meaning
target language	the new language
bilingual dictionary	a dictionary in the target language and one's own language
respond	answer
physically	using one's body
phrases	combinations of words
academic material	reading or listening passages on academic content (such as business, biology, or history)

EXPANSION ACTIVITY: Write Sentences

- ❍ Have students create new sentences using the words from Activity B.
- ❍ Put students in pairs to read their sentences to a partner.
- ❍ Call on students to read sentences to the class.

C. Application

- ❍ Go over the directions.
- ❍ Have students work individually to check the activities they do in class.
- ❍ Put students in small groups to discuss which methods and techniques they like.
- ❍ Call on representatives from each group to share their ideas with the class.

ANSWER KEY

Answers will vary.

CRITICAL THINKING STRATEGY: Synthesizing

- ❍ Go over the material in the box.

D. Practice: Synthesizing

- ❍ Go over the directions.
- ❍ Put students in small groups to complete the chart.
- ❍ Call on students to share their ideas with the class.

ANSWER KEY

Facts about the Brain	Methods
The brain needs a rich environment. The main characteristic of a rich environment is stimulation.	the Natural Approach
The best way to grow a better brain" is to do problem-solving.	the lexical approach; the content-based approach
We remember best in chunks," not bits.	the lexical approach; the Natural Approach
The brain and body remember together.	TP"

TOEFL® iBT Tip

TOEFL iBT TIP 4: The TOEFL iBT tests the ability to read a passage, listen to a lecture related to that passage, and then write in response to a question based on the two stimuli. This integrated writing skill requires students to think critically about material that they have read, interpret that information and relate it to a lecture, then present ideas in essay format.

- ❍ Point out that the *Synthesizing* strategy and activity can be further applied in the next parts of this chapter: *The Mechanics of Writing* and *Academic Writing*.
- ❍ On the TOEFL iBT, students will have 20 minutes to plan and write a response.

On the TOEFL iBT this question may appear in the following format:

Summarize the points made in the lecture you just heard, explaining how they {compare to, cast doubt on, refute} points made in the reading. You may refer to the reading passage as you write.

E. Journal Writing

❍ Go over the directions.
❍ Have students choose one topic.
❍ Explain that this is a quick-writing activity and does not have to be perfect. Point out that journal writing can be a warm-up to a more structured writing assignment, helping to generate ideas.
❍ Have students write. Set a time limit of five minutes.
❍ Put students in pairs to read or talk about their writing.

Website Research

❍ For additional information on the brain and memory, you could direct students to these websites:
- Brain Power, Liberty Science Center (http://www.lsc.org/online_science/brainpower/brainpower.html)
- The Memory Exhibition, Exploratorium (http://www.exploratorium.edu/memory)

❍ For additional information on language learning methods, you could direct students to these websites:
- Lingual Links: A brief survey of language learning methods (http://www.sil.org/lingualinks/LANGUAGE LEARNING/WaysToApproachLanguageLearning/ABriefSurveyOfLanguageLearning.htm)
- Language Teaching Methods—FIS, Parent Information (http://esl.fis.edu/parents/advice/method.htm)
- Teaching Methods: Foreign language study and the brain, University of Idaho (http://ivc.uidaho.edu/flbrain/learning.htm)

PART 4 THE MECHANICS OF WRITING, PAGES 43–45

❍ Go over the directions.

Using the Word *Or*

❍ Go over the information in the box about using the word *or.*
❍ Point out that students may have learned that *or* is used to present choices. This is another way to use *or.*

A. Practice: Using the Word *Or*

❍ Go over the directions.
❍ Have students combine the sentences using *or.*
❍ Put students in pairs to check their answers.
❍ Call on volunteers to write the sentences on the board or read them out loud to the class.

ANSWER KEY

1. I don't know Maria or Jen.
2. David didn't make mistakes in grammar or spelling.
3. We don't need to read Chapter 5 or Chapter 6.
4. In that class, they don't practice listening or speaking.
5. Julia doesn't have the class notes or know the assignment.

EXPANSION ACTIVITY: Pair Share

❍ Put students in pairs.
❍ Ask students to talk with their partners for three minutes and find at least five things they have in common that they don't like or don't do.
❍ Have students write three sentences using *or* to talk about what they and their partners don't like or don't do.
❍ Call on students to read sentences to the class.

Punctuation with the Word *But*

❍ Go over the information in the box. Ask: *What kind of ideas do we show with* but? *When do we use a comma with* but?

B. Practice: Punctuation with the Word *But*

❍ Go over the directions.
❍ Read the first pair of sentences and elicit ways to combine the two using *but* (*I studied French but not Greek.*). Point out that there is no comma because *but* doesn't join complete sentences. If students combine the sentences without reduction (*I studied French, but I didn't study Greek.*), they will need a comma.
❍ Have students combine the sentences.
❍ Have students check their answers with a partner.
❍ Go over the answers with the class.

ANSWER KEY

1. I studied French but not Greek. *OR* I studied French, but I didn't study Greek.
2. We worked on vocabulary, but we didn't work on grammar. *OR* We worked on vocabulary but not on grammar.
3. Emma did Chapter 5, but she didn't do Chapter 6. *OR* Emma did Chapter 5 but not Chapter 6.
4. We don't practice listening or speaking, but that isn't a problem for me.
5. Some students think this is a problem, but I don't.

EXPANSION ACTIVITY: Pair Share Variation

- Put students in pairs.
- Ask students to talk with their partners for three minutes and find at least five ways they differ.
- Have students write three sentences using *but* to talk about how they and their partners are different.
- Call on students to read sentences to the class.

Words in Phrases: Words after Prepositions

- Go over the information in the box.
- Ask comprehension questions such as: *What kind of word usually follows a preposition? The preposition* to? *What is one verb that is often followed by* to? *What follows the preposition* by?
- Point out that remembering words in phrases is using chunks, as was suggested in the reading about the brain.

C. Practice: Words after Prepositions

- Go over the directions.
- If necessary, review the rules for spelling *-ing* words, or direct students to page 168 in the student book for review.
- Have students fill in the blanks with the correct forms of the verbs in parentheses.
- Have students check their answers with a partner.
- Go over the answers with the class.

ANSWER KEY

1. learning; 2. having; 3. practice; 4. synthesize; 5. learning; 6. learn; 7. reading; 8. writing; 9. be; 10. do

EXPANSION ACTIVITY: Interview

- Write the following phrases on the board:
  focus on
  worry about
  important to
  need to
  interested in
- Explain that students will be interviewing a partner about their ideas regarding education and learning.
- Model the activity. Call on a student and ask a question using one of the phrases (*What do you worry about the most in this class?*).
- Have students work individually to write three questions, with each question using one of the phrases on the board. Walk around the room to monitor the activity and provide help as needed.
- Call on a few students to read one of their questions aloud.
- Put students in pairs to practice asking and answering the questions.
- Call on students to tell the class about their partners.

D. Practice: Answering Questions with *How*?

- Go over the directions and the example. Point out that the answer uses *by* + a gerund.
- Have students answer the questions using the correct forms of the phrases in parentheses.
- Have students compare their answers with a partner.
- Go over the answers with the class.

ANSWER KEY

1. They learn a new language by translating it.
2. They learn vocabulary by memorizing lists of new words.
3. They show they understand the teacher by following commands.
4. They learn vocabulary by reading a lot.
5. They learn new words by reading them, practicing them, and using them in discussion.

EXPANSION ACTIVITY: Find a Match

- Distribute two index cards or slips of paper to each student.
- Model the activity. Start a sentence based on the readings from Part 2 or Part 3: *In the lexical approach, students learn how to use new words by...* Elicit a completion (*noticing groups of words*).
- Have students look at the readings from Parts 2 and 3 to write a sentence starter about the material on one index card. Remind them to end the sentence starter with the word *by.*
- Collect and redistribute the cards.
- Have students write a completion for the sentence starter card they received on their second index card.
- Call on students to read their completed sentences aloud.
- For a variation, again collect all starter cards in one pile. Collect the completion cards in the other.
- Distribute the cards so that each student has one card from each pile.
- Have students stand and walk around the room to find the cards that make their sentences complete.

Using the Word *Because*

- Go over the information in the box about using the word *because.*

Grammar Note:

- Some of your students may know that *because* can start a sentence (*Because they need to learn the language, they're taking the class.*). Although that structure is correct, it is not the form that is practiced here. Remind students to answer these questions with *because* in the middle of the sentence.

E. Practice: Using the Word *Because*

- Go over the directions.
- Read the first question aloud and elicit possible answers (*I like the Natural Approach because I like to talk to other students.*). Make sure students restate the question to begin the sentence and use the word *because.*
- Have students write answers to the questions.
- Put students in pairs to practice asking and answering the questions.
- Call on students to tell the class one of their partner's answers.

ANSWER KEY

Answers will vary.

F. Review: Editing a Paragraph

- Go over the directions.
- Have students find and correct the eight mistakes. Have them check their answers with a partner.
- Go over the answers with the class.

ANSWER KEY

I think a good way to ~~learning~~ learn a new language is by ~~use~~ using a combination of methods~~/~~ ~~B~~ because there is something good about each one. For example, I like the idea of focus[ing] on communication in the Natural Approach[,] but I like the lexical approach, too. Also, I need [to] study academic material~~/~~ because I hope to go to college. That's why the content-based method is good.

TOEFL® iBT Tip

TOEFL iBT TIP 5: Both the integrated and independent essays of the TOEFL iBT will be scored based on how well the examinee completes the overall writing task. However, the writing section also requires that the essay follow the conventions of spelling, punctuation, and layout.

- Point out that the editing activities in *The Mechanics of Writing* part of this chapter will help students improve their grammar, usage, spelling, and the overall flow of their essays.

PART 5 ACADEMIC WRITING, PAGES 46–50

Writing Assignment

❍ Go over the directions.

Model

❍ Have students read the six steps of the example.
❍ Direct students' attention to Step A of the example, and ask: *What topic did the student choose?* Elicit reasons why the grammar-translation method is a good way to study Latin.
❍ Direct students' attention to Step B. Ask: *What questions did the student use to get ideas?* Elicit other ways to gather ideas.
❍ Direct students' attention to Step C. Elicit examples of how the student expanded upon the notes in Step B. Ask students if they notice any mistakes.
❍ Have students read the paragraph in Step D and ask how it is different from the sentences in C. Point out or elicit that the first sentence states the topic of the paragraph.
❍ Direct students' attention to Step E. Ask: *How many mistakes did the writer circle in the paragraph in Step D? What are they?*
❍ Have students read the paragraph in Step F. Ask: *How did the writer correct the mistakes?*

Your Turn

❍ Go over the directions.
❍ Have students read Step A and choose a language and method.

WRITING STRATEGY: Getting Ideas

❍ Go over the information in the box.
❍ Ask: *What are some ways you can get ideas for your paragraph? What is an important skill to have in writing essay exams?*

TOEFL® iBT Tip

TOEFL iBT TIP 6: The integrated writing skill on the TOEFL iBT requires students to think critically about material that they have read, interpret that information and relate it to a lecture, then present ideas in essay format.

❍ Point out that *Step B, Getting Ideas* corresponds to a strategy they will need to use when writing their essays. They will be able to get ideas from the reading passage or from the notes that they take from the lecture. Students will need to summarize and present ideas in an original way. They are encouraged to refer to the reading passage to stimulate and expand on their ideas.

(**Your Turn**, *continued*)
❍ Have students answer the questions in Step B.
❍ Put students in pairs according to language chosen and topic, if possible. Have students share their ideas. Walk around the room to monitor the activity and provide help as needed.
❍ Have students complete Steps C and D. If you want to have your students practice peer editing skills, have them exchange paragraphs with a partner and comment on mistakes or other problems.
❍ Ask students to edit their paragraphs (Step E) and then rewrite (Step F).
❍ Collect the paragraphs.

EXPANSION ACTIVITY: Which One Is It?

❍ Have students rewrite or edit their paragraphs to remove any mention of the name of the method discussed.
❍ Call on students to read their paragraphs aloud. Ask the class to guess which method is being discussed.

Unit 1 Vocabulary Workshop

❍ Have students review vocabulary from Chapters 1 and 2.

A. Matching

❍ Go over the directions.
❍ Have students write the correct letters on the lines to match the definitions with the words.
❍ Go over the answers.

ANSWER KEY
1. d; 2. g; 3. j; 4. a; 5. e; 6. h; 7. f; 8. c; 9. b; 10. i

B. True or False?

❍ Go over the directions.
❍ Have students fill in the correct bubbles.
❍ Go over the answers.

ANSWER KEY
1. F; 2. T; 3. F; 4. T; 5. T; 6. F; 7. T; 8. T

C. Words in Phrases: Prepositions

❍ Go over the directions.
❍ Have students fill in the blanks with the correct prepositions.
❍ Go over the answers.

ANSWER KEY
1. to; from; of; on; 2. on; about; of; to

D. Which Word Doesn't Belong?

❍ Go over the directions.
❍ Have students cross out the word that doesn't belong in each row.
❍ Go over the answers.

ANSWER KEY
crossed out:
1. emotion; 2. role; 3. chunks; 4. assign; 5. English class; 6. personality; 7. easy; 8. material

UNIT 2 BUSINESS

Unit Opener, page 53

- ❍ Direct students' attention to the photo on page 53. Ask questions: *What do you see in the picture? What is the man doing? Where do you think he is?*
- ❍ Brainstorm ideas for what the unit will include and write students' ideas on the board.

CHAPTER 3 DECIDING ON A CAREER

In this chapter, students will explore how to find happiness in a career. They will answer a questionnaire and will read about how people choose a career. Students will read about the ideas of Martin E.P. Seligman, who has written many books on optimism and finding happiness. Students will be introduced to Mihaly Csikszentmihaly and his discoveries about happiness. Students will also see how to use their talents, passions, and strengths to choose a career. These topics will prepare students to write about their ideas of the perfect career.

VOCABULARY

acquire	aware of	encouragement	mentors	role models
activities	career	experts	moments	smoothly
admire	commercials	gender	moral characteristics	talent
advertising	counselor	however	passion	unfortunately
advice	crazy about	involves	passive	wealth
ancient	the distant past	major	profession	
archaeologist	don't matter	mentally	psychology	

READING STRATEGIES

Guessing the Meanings of New Words: Commas
Guessing the Meanings of New Words:
  Finding Meaning in Another Part of the Sentence
  or in Another Sentence
Understanding Pronoun References
Understanding Punctuation: Italics and Quotation Marks

CRITICAL THINKING STRATEGIES

Applying Information (Part 2)
Thinking of Solutions (Part 2)
Interpreting Information (Part 3)
Synthesizing (Part 3)
Note: The strategy in bold is highlighted in the student book.

MECHANICS

The Future Tense
Possibility: *May* and *Might*
Using the Word *Or*
Using *Enjoy* and *Involve*
Adverbial Conjunctions
Words in Phrases: Words for Work

WRITING STRATEGY

Writing Complete Sentences

CHAPTER 3 Deciding on a Career

Chapter 3 Opener, page 55

- Direct students' attention to the photo. Ask them what is happening in the photo.
- Have students discuss the four questions. This can be done in pairs, in small groups, or as a class.
- Check students' predictions of the chapter topic.

PART 1 INTRODUCTION CAREER QUESTIONNAIRE, PAGES 56–58

Before Reading

Thinking Ahead

- Have students look at the photos. Ask questions such as: *What jobs do you see here? Which do you think are more interesting? Which one do you think is more fun? Which one do you think pays the most?*
- Put students in pairs to answer the questions.
- Call on students to share their answers with the class.

ANSWER KEY

Answers will vary.

EXPANSION ACTIVITY: Value Line-Up

- Have a group of students come to the front of the room.
- Tell these students that they should form a continuum to reflect their opinions about jobs. Identify one side of the room as *not important to me*, and the other side as *very important to me*. Explain that you will say a characteristic and students should move to the place that indicates how important the characteristic is for them.
- Say a characteristic of a job (e.g., *work with people*) and have students move. Call on a couple of students to explain their position.
- Continue with one or two other characteristics (e.g., *solve problems, work independently, be creative*).
- Call another group of students to the board and repeat with other characteristics (*work with numbers, make a lot of money, do a lot of different things*).
- Ask questions about the activity: *What characteristics were important to people? Does everyone have the same values?*

Reading

- Have students look at the reading. Ask: *What type of reading is this?* Go over the directions.
- Have students mark their answers to the questions as they read the questionnaire silently, or have students answer questions as you play the audio program.

EXPANSION ACTIVITY: A Favorite Work Experience

- Model the activity. Tell the class about a work experience (paid or volunteer) that you really enjoyed and why.
- Put students in pairs to share a work experience that they really enjoyed and why.
- Call on students to tell the class about their partner's favorite work experience.

After Reading

A. Extension

- Go over the directions and the examples.
- Have students write sentences using the questionnaire.

ANSWER KEY

Answers will vary.

B. Talk About It

❍ Go over the directions and the example.
❍ Put students in small groups.
❍ Have students read their sentences from Activity A. Have students talk about what job might be good for each person.
❍ Call on students to share their ideas with the class.

ANSWER KEY
Answers will vary.

EXPANSION ACTIVITY: Ranking

❍ Point out that sometimes we like many things, and we may need to prioritize in order to make decisions about careers.
❍ Model the activity. Using the questionnaire from the reading, tell students what you like the most in Question 1 (*I like ideas the most.*), what you enjoy the most in Question 2 (*I enjoy languages the most.*), and where you are the most happy (*I am the happiest when I am in a library.*).
❍ Have students rank the items in Questions 1–3, writing 1 next to the thing they like or enjoy the most, or where they are most happy.
❍ Put students in pairs to share their ideas.

PART 2 GENERAL INTEREST READING WHERE AM I, AND WHERE AM I GOING?, PAGES 59–63

Before Reading

A. Thinking Ahead

❍ Go over the directions and questions.
❍ Put students in pairs to answer the questions.
❍ Call on students to share their ideas with the class.

ANSWER KEY
Answers will vary.

CRITICAL THINKING STRATEGY: Applying Information

❍ Point out to students that the bold-faced words may indicate words that are new to students, but that they can apply their knowledge about guessing the meanings of new words.

Culture Notes:

❍ You may want to point out that the role of work may be more important in some cultures than in others.
❍ Ask students how important work is in their culture. Ask what kind of work is most valued.
❍ In the United States, it is common to ask people about their jobs when you first meet them.

B. Vocabulary Preparation

❍ Go over the directions and the example. Have students look at the definitions. Explain unfamiliar terms if necessary.
❍ Have students match the rest of the definitions to the words in blue by writing the letters on the lines next to the sentences.
❍ Have students check their answers with a partner.
❍ Go over the answers with the class.

ANSWER KEY
1. f; 2. b; 3. c; 4. a; 5. d; 6. e

EXPANSION ACTIVITY: Sentence Practice

- ❍ Tell students they have one minute to review the vocabulary.
- ❍ Write the six vocabulary words from Activity B on the board. Have students close their books.
- ❍ Set a time limit of two minutes. Have students write sentences using all six vocabulary words. Students should try to use all the vocabulary words in the fewest number of sentences they can while still using the words correctly.
- ❍ Call on students to read their sentences to the class.

READING STRATEGY: Guessing the Meanings of New Words: Commas

- ❍ Go over the information in the box.
- ❍ Point out that sometimes commas come in pairs. In that case, the definition or explanation is between the two commas. If the explanation is at the end of a sentence, there is only one comma.

C. Guessing the Meanings of New Words: Commas

- ❍ Go over the directions.
- ❍ Have students look over the first passage. Elicit an example of a definition set off by commas *(major)*.

TOEFL® iBT Tip

TOEFL iBT TIP 1: The TOEFL iBT tests the ability to determine the meaning of words in context.

- ❍ Point out that the strategy and activity for *Guessing the Meanings of New Words: Commas* will help students improve their vocabulary for the TOEFL iBT. By identifying words that are in *apposition to* (next to) other words, words sometimes placed after the comma, students will be able to apply these definitions or explanations toward further understanding the concepts presented in the text.

- ❍ Useful vocabulary words or phrases from the reading include the following: *a discoverer of people and places from the past, a passion for teaching,* and *a real talent.*

On the TOEFL iBT this question appears in the following format:

The phrase ______________ in the passage is closest in meaning to…

Reading

- ❍ Go over the directions and the questions.
- ❍ Have students read the passage silently, or play the audio program as students follow along.

After Reading

A. Check Your Understanding

- ❍ Go over the directions.
- ❍ Have students match the person's name with the correct situation. Encourage them to review the reading if necessary.
- ❍ Go over the answers with the class.

ANSWER KEY

1. b; 2. a; 3. d; 4. c

B. Vocabulary Check

- ❍ Direct students' attention to the words in the box. Say each word and have students repeat.
- ❍ Go over the directions and the example.
- ❍ Have students fill in the blanks and then check their answers with a partner.
- ❍ Go over the answers with the class.

ANSWER KEY

1. advertising; 2. archaeologist; 3. the distant past; 4. aware of; 5. passion; 6. talent

C. Making Connections: Parts 1 and 2

- ❍ Go over the directions.
- ❍ Have students choose one of the four people from the reading and answer the questionnaire as if they were that person.
- ❍ Put students in pairs to talk about how they answered the questions for the person they chose.
- ❍ Have students share ideas with the class.

ANSWER KEY
Answers will vary.

EXPANSION ACTIVITY: Who Am I?

- Explain the activity: a student will be one of the four people from the reading. Classmates should ask the student *yes/no* questions based on the questionnaire to figure out who the person is (*Do you like animals? Are you good with plants?*). Tell students they must receive five *yes* answers before they can make a guess.
- Walk around the room and whisper to each student the name of one of the four people in the reading. Have each student complete the questionnaire for the person you assigned. Remind students to answer every question.
- Call on a volunteer to come to the front of the room.
- Have the other students ask *yes/no* questions based on the questionnaire.
- Continue until students correctly name the person.
- Repeat with other volunteers.

CRITICAL THINKING STRATEGY: Thinking of Solutions

- Go over the information in the box.

D. Extension

- Go over the directions and the examples.
- Review the use of *should* and *shouldn't* if necessary. Remind students that the simple form of the verb does not change.
- Put students in small groups to practice giving advice to each person from the reading.
- Call on students to share their advice with the class.

EXPANSION ACTIVITY: Dear Career Coach

- Have students write short letters about themselves or someone they know and their career concerns. Suggest they follow the examples in the reading on pages 60–61.
- Put students in pairs to read their letters and revise if necessary.
- Call on students to read their letters to the class. Elicit advice. Remind students to use *should* and *shouldn't* to give advice.

PART  ACADEMIC READING, THE JOY OF WORK?, PAGES 63–70

Before Reading

A. Thinking Ahead

- Go over the directions.
- Have students stand and walk around the room, and ask 10 classmates for opinions. Remind them to write their classmates' answers in the chart.
- When students have finished, ask for volunteers to tell the class about one classmate's opinion.

ANSWER KEY
Answers will vary.

CRITICAL THINKING STRATEGY: Interpreting Information

- Point out that this activity is similar to the first questionnaire in that it is a way to find out information from many people. Explain or elicit that answers to surveys or questionnaires can be grouped to provide numerical information. Point out to students that grouping results is useful because it can show patterns or trends.
- You could use the following expansion activity (*Report the Data*) to help students practice interpreting information.

EXPANSION ACTIVITY: Report the Data

- Have students look at the opinions their classmates gave and see if there are any answers that are similar. For example, if one student answered *They work long hours*, and another said *They think about work all the time*, you might notice that both answers are about the amount of time spent on work.

❍ Have students group any answers that are similar and give the category a label (*amount of time spent on work*). They should notice which categories of answers were more frequently reported.
❍ Put students in pairs to talk about what they noticed in the answers.
❍ Ask questions: *What kind of characteristics did most people talk about? How would you describe people who love their work? What do they have in common? Are these characteristics you can develop?*

B. Vocabulary Preparation

❍ Go over the directions.
❍ Have students match the definitions to the words, and then check their answers with a partner.
❍ Go over the answers with the class.

ANSWER KEY

1. e; 2. d; 3. f; 4. c; 5. b; 6. a; 7. g

EXPANSION ACTIVITY: Beanbag Toss

❍ Give students a minute to review the vocabulary words from Activity B.
❍ Call on a student and toss a ball or beanbag as you say a word from the activity (*acquire*). The student should provide the definition as he or she catches the ball or beanbag (*get*) and tosses it back to you.
❍ Continue until all the words have been defined. You may repeat another round for more practice.
❍ As a variation, call on students and give the definition and elicit the vocabulary word. Continue until all vocabulary words have been matched to a definition.

READING STRATEGY: Guessing the Meanings of New Words: Finding Meaning in Another Part of the Sentence or in Another Sentence

❍ Go over the information in the box. Ask: *Where can the definition of a new word sometimes be found?*

C. Guessing the Meanings of New Words

❍ Go over the directions.
❍ Have students locate the word *passive* in the first paragraph and elicit the meaning from the words nearby. Remind students to look for meanings around the new words as they read.

TOEFL® iBT Tip

TOEFL iBT TIP 2: The TOEFL iBT tests the ability to understand key words contained within a text.

❍ Point out that the strategy and activity for *Guessing the Meanings of New Words* will help students improve their vocabulary for the TOEFL iBT. Locating key words in a sentence and linking them to meanings in another sentence will help students build vocabulary and improve their reading skills.

❍ The test may also require students to determine how or why the author uses a particular phrase to define a term or describe something.

On the TOEFL iBT this question may appear in the following format:

In stating __________, the author means that ...

Reading

❍ Go over the directions and the question.
❍ Have students read the passage silently, or play the audio program and have students follow along silently.

Academic Notes:

❍ You may want to point out that academic readings often have key terms. Explain that a key term is important to understanding the material. Point out that just because a word is unfamiliar doesn't mean it is important. Key terms are those we must understand in order to identify main ideas.
❍ Have students preview the reading and identify one key term. (*Flow* is probably the easiest one to find. Students will have a chance to identify other key terms in the Expansion Activity *Key Terms* on page 34 of the Teacher's Edition.)

After Reading

A. Check Your Understanding

❍ Go over the directions.
❍ Have students check the correct answers. Encourage students to review the reading if necessary and then compare answers with a partner.
❍ Go over the answers with the class.

ANSWER KEY

Check: people to give us advice and encouragement, our talents, our passions, our strengths

EXPANSION ACTIVITY: Key Terms

❍ Point out that this article has several key terms, as noted previously (see Academic Notes on page 33 of the Teacher's Edition).
❍ Have students reread the passage and highlight the key terms. Ask students to make a note in the margin about each key term.
❍ Put students in pairs to compare their ideas.
❍ Call on students to explain a key term to the class.

ANSWER KEY

Answers may vary, but students should notice the following key terms: *flow, moral characteristics, challenge, focus, control, sense of time, talents, passions and strengths.*

B. Vocabulary Check

❍ Go over the directions.
❍ Have students match the words and phrases with the correct meanings.
❍ Put students in pairs to compare answers.
❍ Go over the answers with the class.

ANSWER KEY

Line Numbers	Word or Term
Line 15	admire
Lines 15–16	role models
Line 20	mentors
Line 33	moral characteristics
Line 51	moments
Line 59	mentally
Lines 63–64	don't matter

EXPANSION ACTIVITY: Summarize

❍ Tell students that a summary is a shorter version of a reading that includes the main ideas but leaves out details.
❍ Ask students to write a one paragraph summary of the reading, using all the words in Activity B.
❍ Put students in pairs to read their summaries.
❍ Call on students to read their summaries aloud to the class.

READING STRATEGY: Understanding Pronoun References

❍ Go over the information in the box. Ask: *What do pronouns take the place of? What are some pronouns?*

C. Practice: Understanding Pronoun References

❍ Go over the directions and the example.
❍ Have students circle each noun and draw an arrow from the pronoun to the noun the pronoun refers to.
❍ Put students in pairs to check their answers.
❍ Go over the answers with the class.

ANSWER KEY

1. Why do (adults) hate their work? Why don't **they** choose fun jobs?
2. (Mentors) give us advice. **They** give us encouragement.
3. Everyone has certain (strengths.) How are **they** different from talents?
4. This (psychologist) studies a wonderful (condition.) **He** calls **it** "flow."
5. (Flow) does not last long. **It** "visits you for a few minutes."

TOEFL® iBT Tip

TOEFL iBT Tip 3: The TOEFL iBT measures the ability to identify the relationships between pronouns and their *antecedents* (words that come before) or *postcedents* (words that follow them) in a passage.

❍ Point out that the strategy and activity for *Understanding Pronoun References* will help students improve their ability to correctly identify and link pronouns and nouns on the TOEFL iBT.

On the TOEFL iBT this question may appear in the following format:

The word ________ *in the passage refers to …*

EXPANSION ACTIVITY: Using a Graphic Organizer

❍ Photocopy the Black Line Master *Graphic Organizer* on page BLM 4 and distribute to students.
❍ Have students complete the graphic organizer with information from the reading. For a challenge, have students review the reading and then complete the graphic organizer from memory.
❍ Put students in pairs to compare outlines.
❍ Have volunteers recreate the graphic organizer on the board.

ANSWER KEY

The Jo of Work

Find the Right People	**Discover Your Talents, Passions and Strengths**	**Characteristics of Flow**
1. role models	1. talents: things we're good at	1. challenge and possibility
2. mentors	2. passions: things we love	2. focus
	3. strengths: moral characteristics	3. control
		4. sense of time

READING STRATEGY: Understanding Punctuation: Italics and Quotation Marks

❍ Go over the information in the box.
❍ Ask: *When do we use italics? When do we use quotation marks? What type of punctuation can show stress?*

D. Practice: Understanding Punctuation: Italics and Quotation Marks

❍ Go over the directions.
❍ Have students circle words in italics and quotation marks and write the information where appropriate on the lines.
❍ Go over the answers with the class.

ANSWER KEY

Titles:
Secrets of People Who Love their Work
Authentic Happiness
Flow: The Psychology of Optimal Experience

Person's words:
Why do adults hate their work?
Why don't they choose fun jobs?
I want to be like them.
They are the people who show us how to dream.
You can do it!
Don't give up.
cheeks sent me high
visits you for a few minutes

ANSWER KEY, continued

almost identical
What is a good life?

Emphasis:
fun, active, doing, doing something, love, choose, anything, all, flows, both, possible, only

TOEFL® iBT Tip

TOEFL iBT TIP 4: Both the integrated and independent essays of the TOEFL iBT will be scored based on how well the examinee completes the overall writing task. However, the writing section also requires that the essay follow the conventions of spelling, punctuation, and layout.

- ❍ Point out that the punctuation activities in *Understanding Punctuation: Italics and Quotation Marks* will help students understand vocabulary, quoted information, and titles that the author uses in a passage.
- ❍ Remind students that they will also be able to apply these strategies to writing their essays, particularly when they are required to paraphrase or quote parts of a text.

CRITICAL THINKING STRATEGY: Synthesizing

- ❍ Remind students that when they put together information from different sources, they are synthesizing (as in Activity E).

E. Review: Synthesis

- ❍ Go over the directions.
- ❍ Have students complete the chart and then compare answers with a partner.
- ❍ Go over the answers with the class.

ANSWER KEY

Person	Talents	Passions	Strengths
Tiffany G.	problem solving	art, music, science	problem solving
Chris M.	good with words, people skills	own business, family and friends	ability to work in a group, honesty
Brian F.	problem solving, ability to be careful	distant past	gratitude, problem solving, interest in the world
Diego C.	sports, business, foreign languages	travel	interest in the world, honesty

TOEFL® iBT Tip

TOEFL iBT TIP 5: The TOEFL iBT tests the ability to create a mental framework, like a category chart or an outline, in order to organize the major points or important details in a passage.

- ❍ Point out that activity *Synthesizing* (Activity E) helps students to organize the information that they have read in the passage and connect and organize that information.

On the TOEFL iBT this question may appear in the form of a schematic table in which examinees must match appropriate statements with categories discussed in the passage. Partial credit is given depending on how many correct answers there are. There may be five to seven key items tested in this type of question, with each question worth three to four points.

 **EXPANSION ACTIVITY: Online Research**

- ❍ Have students find the website for the VIA Classification of Character Strengths (http://www.authentichappiness.org/Strengths.html) to view information about the 24 strengths.
- ❍ Have students add information for the four people to the chart in Activity E based on the information they find on the website.
- ❍ Ask students to make a chart and list their own personal talents, passions, and strengths.
- ❍ Have students share with a partner.

F. Journal Writing

- ❍ Go over the directions. Have students select a topic.
- ❍ Explain that this is a quick-writing activity and does not have to be perfect. Point out that journal writing can be a warm-up to a more structured writing assignment, helping to generate ideas.
- ❍ Have students write. Set a time limit of five minutes.
- ❍ Put students in pairs to talk about their writing.

 Website Research

- ❍ For additional information on Flow, you could direct students to the following websites:
  - Indianapolis Public Schools—Key Learning Community, Flow Theory (http://www.616.ips.K12.in.us/Theories/Flow/default.aspx)
  - APA monitor—Reaching Flow to Optimize Work and Play (http://www.apa.org/monitor/jul98/joy.html)

PART 4 THE MECHANICS OF WRITING, PAGES 71–74

- ❍ Go over the directions.

The Future Tense/Possibility: *May* and *Might*

- ❍ Go over the information in the boxes about the future tense and *may* and *might*. Ask: *What form of the verb do we use after* going to? *What form do we use after* may *or* might? *When do we use* may *or* might?

A. Practice: The Future Tense

- ❍ Go over the directions.
- ❍ Model the activity. Answer the first question about your own plans for future education (*I am going to take an education class next semester; I might take an English literature class, too.*).
- ❍ Have students write six sentences in response to the questions using *be going to* and *may* or *might*.
- ❍ Put students in pairs to practice asking and answering the questions.
- ❍ Call on volunteers to tell the class about one of their partner's plans.

ANSWER KEY

Answers will vary.

Using the Word *Or*

- ❍ Go over the information in the box about the word *or*.
- ❍ Ask: *When do we use the word* or? *When do we use a comma with* or?

B. Practice: Punctuation with the Word *Or*

- ❍ Go over the directions.
- ❍ Model the activity. Say a sentence about a choice you need to make using the word *or (I'm going to teach here another year, or I may go back to school.)*.
- ❍ Have students write two sentences using the word *or* and then share them with a partner.
- ❍ Call on students to read a sentence to the class.

ANSWER KEY

Answers will vary.

EXPANSION ACTIVITY: This or That

- ❍ Distribute an index card or slip of paper to each student.
- ❍ Have students write a sentence using *may* or *might* to talk about either their own or someone else's future plans (*Maria might go to New York to study fashion.*).
- ❍ Collect the sentences and redistribute, so each student gets another student's card.

- Have students write a new sentence on the card about the subject of the first sentence using *may* or *might* (*Maria might get married.*).
- Collect the cards and redistribute again. Have students combine the sentences on the card using the word *or* (*Maria might go to New York to study fashion, or she might get married.*).
- Call on students to read their sentences to the class, or have volunteers write sentences on the board.

Using *Enjoy* and *Involve*

- Go over the information in the box.
- Ask: *What type of word goes after* enjoy *or* involve?

C. Practice: Using *Enjoy* and *Involve*

- Go over the directions.
- Have students answer the questions and then compare answers with a partner.
- Call on students to answer the questions.

ANSWER KEY

Answers will vary.

Adverbial Conjunctions

- Go over the information in the box.

D. Practice: Adverbial Conjunctions

- Go over the directions.
- Read the first two sentences and elicit a word that could be used to connect them (*First*).
- Have students complete the paragraphs.
- Have students check their answers with a partner.
- Go over the answers with the class.

ANSWER KEY

I love teaching for several reasons. First, I enjoy working with students and with other teachers. Second, I like the challenge. Third, I enjoy making a difference in someone's life. However, I don't like to correct hundreds of exams.

Words in Phrases: Words for Work

- Go over the information in the box.
- Ask comprehension questions such as: *What are examples of professions? What do we call someone who practices medicine? Someone who works in business?*

Vocabulary Notes:

- You may want to point out that certain suffixes, or endings, often indicate fields of work or the people who do the work.
- For example, *–ology* means the study of something. Psychology is the study of the psyche, or the mind. Biology is the study of life, and geology is the study of the Earth. The people who work in these fields are psychologists, biologists, and geologists. Their titles all have the suffix *–ologist.*
- Another suffix frequently used in fields of work is *-ing* (*advertising, acting, writing*). The people who work in these fields are often indicated by a word ending in *–er*, *–or*, or *–ar* (*advertiser, writer, actor*).

E. Practice: Words for Work

- Go over the directions and the examples.
- Have students write two sentences each about three people they know.
- Have students read their sentences to a partner.
- Call on students to read sentences to the class.

ANSWER KEY

Answers will vary.

EXPANSION ACTIVITY: A Mentor

- Review with students the meaning of the word *mentor*.
- Ask students to think of a person who has been a good role model or mentor for them.
- Set a time limit of two minutes. Have students take notes on the person, including his or her profession, talents, passions, and strengths.
- Put students in pairs to talk about their mentors and how the person might have an effect on their own career choices.

- For evaluation purposes, have students prepare a one-minute oral presentation about their mentors. Make a videotape or audiotape of their presentation, and have students evaluate themselves on their correct use of words for work and use of words for possibility.

F. Review: Editing a Paragraph

- Go over the directions.
- Have students find and correct the seven mistakes. Have them check their answers with a partner.
- Go over the answers with the class.

ANSWER KEY

In the future, I ∧am going to work in computer programming/or business. First, I have to choose a college/∧, ~~s~~S second, I need to decide on a major. I'm not sure what to do. I enjoy work∧ing with computers. However∧, I also want to work in my father's company. What can I do? I might work~~ing~~ as a computer programmer in my father's company!

EXPANSION ACTIVITY: Editing Practice

- Photocopy Black Line Master *Editing Practice* on page BLM 5 and distribute it to students.
- Have students edit the paragraph and then compare paragraphs with a partner.
- Go over the corrections with the class.

ANSWER KEY

There are several things to think about if you are going∧to be a language teacher. First∧, you need to enjoy work∧ing with people. Second∧, you should like the language and the people who speak the language. Third∧, this profession involves work∧ing very hard. You may hav∧e ~~ing~~ a lot of students in your class. You might work~~ed~~ long hours preparing for classes. However∧, you may find∧ ~~teacher~~ very rewarding.
education or teaching

PART 5 ACADEMIC WRITING, PAGES 75–79

Writing Assignment

- Go over the directions and the question.

Model

- Have students read the six steps of the example.
- Direct students' attention to Step A of the example, and ask: *What topic did the student choose?*
- Direct students' attention to Step B. Ask: *What questions did the student use to get ideas?* Elicit other ways to gather ideas.
- Direct students' attention to Step C. Elicit examples of the information the student included, and why the information is helpful. Point out that the student used *enjoy* and *involve* in examples. Ask students if they notice any mistakes.
- Have students read the paragraph in Step D of the example. Have students underline the transition words the writer used to connect the ideas.
- Direct students' attention to Step E. Ask: *How many mistakes did the writer circle in the paragraph in step D? What are they?*
- Have students read the paragraph in Step F. Ask: *How did the writer correct the mistakes?*

Your Turn

- Have students read Step A and choose a topic.
- Have students answer the questions in Step B. You may want to put students in pairs to discuss their ideas.

WRITING STRATEGY: Writing Complete Sentences

- Remind students that they have already practiced the writing strategies of choosing a topic and getting ideas.
- Go over the information in the box. Ask: *What are two things that every complete sentence must have? How does a sentence begin? How does it end? What are some words we can use to put two complete sentences together?*

(**Your Turn**, *continued*)

- Have students complete Step C.
- Put students in pairs to exchange sentences. Remind students to check for subjects, verbs, capital letters, ending punctuation, connecting words, and commas.
- Have students complete Step D. If you want to have your students practice peer editing skills, have them exchange paragraphs with a partner and comment on mistakes or other problems.
- Ask students to edit their paragraphs (Step E) and then rewrite (Step F).
- Collect student paragraphs.

TOEFL® iBT Tip

TOEFL iBT TIP 6: Both the integrated and independent essays of the TOEFL iBT will be scored based on how well the examinee completes the overall writing task. However, the writing section also requires that the essay follow the conventions of spelling, punctuation, and layout.

- Remind students that they will need to write full sentences and punctuate the sentences correctly.

EXPANSION ACTIVITY: Complete Practice

- Put students in pairs.
- Have students take turns asking the questions in Step B to conduct a partner interview. Tell students to take notes on their partner's answers.
- Have students use their notes to write complete sentences about their partner's career choice.
- Call on students to tell the class about their partner's choice.

UNIT 2 BUSINESS

CHAPTER 4 MARKETING ACROSS TIME AND SPACE

In this chapter, students will read about the marketing of products. Students will first find out how titles are chosen for movies that are exported to other countries. The readings refer to American movies such as *Along Came Polly, You've Got Mail, Out of Africa, 101 Dalmations, Legally Blonde, As Good As It Gets,* and *Deep Impact*, as well as international movies such as *Amores Perros* and *Tampopo*. Students will read about advertising throughout history, including the first package ads in China in the 13th century, Japanese handbills in the late 19th century, and the short Internet movies created by companies today. Finally, students will get an overview of advertising in today's world. These topics will prepare students to write a paragraph describing a commercial.

VOCABULARY

appeals to	fan	income	packaging	town criers
attract	here to stay	irritating	personalize	trademark
belong to	highlights	junk	product image	values
clicking a button	high-performance	market	qualities	
effective	image	name brand	reflect	
fact of life	improve	outdoor displays	specific	

READING STRATEGIES

Guessing the Meanings of New Words:
Adjective Clauses with *Who* and *That*
Making Notes
Guessing the Meanings of New Words: Colons
Finding Examples
Recognizing Word Forms

CRITICAL THINKING STRATEGIES

Evaluation (Part 2)
Synthesizing (Part 3)

MECHANICS

The Present Continuous Tense
Review: The Simple Present Tense
Subject-Verb Agreement
Showing Order
Adjectives
Adverbs
Words in Phrases: *It Is, There Is/Are*

WRITING STRATEGY

Writing a Paragraph

CHAPTER 4 Marketing Across Time and Space

Chapter 4 Opener, page 81

❍ Direct students' attention to the photo. Ask them what they see in the photo.
❍ Have students discuss the four questions. This can be done in pairs, in small groups, or as a class.
❍ Check students' predictions of the chapter topic.

PART 1 INTRODUCTION SELLING MOVIES, PAGES 82–85

Before Reading

Thinking Ahead

❍ Have students look at the photo. Ask questions: *Where are they? What are they doing? How do you know?*
❍ Go over the directions. Direct students' attention to the photos on pages 83 and 95.
❍ Put students in pairs to answer the questions.
❍ Call on students to share their answers with the class.

ANSWER KEY

Answers will vary.

EXPANSION ACTIVITY: Category Sort

❍ Have students stand. Tell students that you will ask a question, and they should sort themselves so that they are standing with classmates who have the same or similar answers.
❍ Ask: *What was the last movie you saw?* Allow students a minute or two to sort themselves. Students should ask questions and move around until they are in the right group. Walk around to monitor the activity and provide help if needed.
❍ Continue the activity with different questions. Use the questions from the *Thinking Ahead* activity, or create your own *(What type of movie do you like the least? How often do you go to the movies? Who is your favorite actor? Who is your favorite director?).*
❍ This should be a fast-paced activity once students understand the process.

Reading

❍ Go over the directions and the question.
❍ Have students read the passage silently, or have students follow along silently as you play the audio program.
❍ Ask students why movies sometimes have different titles in different countries.

Culture Notes:

❍ *Along Came Polly* (2004) is an American movie about an obsessively organized insurance salesman who falls in love with an old classmate after his new wife leaves him.
❍ *You've Got Mail* (1998) is about two rival bookstore owners who fall in love through email.
❍ *Out of Africa* (1985) is about a romance between a plantation owner and a big-game hunter in Africa. The movie is based on the book by Isak Dinesen.
❍ *101 Dalmations* (1961) is a Disney animated movie that was remade as a live action feature in 1996. It's about two dalmations whose puppies are kidnapped. The dalmations, with other animal friends, begin a search and rescue.
❍ *Legally Blonde* (2001) tells the story of a blonde sorority girl who is surprisingly successful in law school.
❍ *As Good As It Gets* (1997) is about an obsessive compulsive writer who falls in love with a waitress.
❍ *Deep Impact* (1998) is about an asteroid coming to earth and the preparations different people make in their lives as they wait for it.
❍ *Amores Perros* (2000) tells three stories all linked by a terrible car accident.
❍ *Tampopo* (1985) is about a woman named Tampopo, who owns a noodle shop and seeks to make the best noodles amidst other adventures. The movie's title is the Japanese word for dandelion, a weed and flower.

EXPANSION ACTIVITY: Making Connections

- ❍ Remind students that they have practiced making connections between ideas in earlier chapters, including understanding pronouns and synthesizing. Tell students to use those skills in this activity.
- ❍ Photocopy the sentences below from the reading (lines 15–28) and cut them into strips. Make enough so each pair of students has a set.
- ❍ Have students form pairs. Distribute a set of the sentence strips to each pair and have students reconstruct the paragraphs with books closed.
- ❍ Go over the answers with the class.
- ❍ In a variation, dictate the sentences from one of the paragraphs in the reading to the students out of order. Ask students to put the sentences back in the original order.

Often the new title of the movie is identical to the original one.

An example is the American film *Along Came Polly.*

In Germany, the title was ... *und dann kam Polly,* a direct translation.

However, sometimes the movie makers do not translate original titles directly.

Instead, they make changes that "sound" good in the foreign language.

For example, the American movie *You've Got Mail* was *Yū gatto mēru* in Japan.

The new spelling of the words shows how the English title sounds to Japanese ears.

After Reading

A. Check Your Understanding

- ❍ Go over the directions.
- ❍ Have students fill in *T* or *F* next to each sentence.
- ❍ Have students check their answers with a partner.
- ❍ Go over the answers with the class. For additional practice, have students correct the false statements.

ANSWER KEY

1. F; 2. T; 3. T; 4. T; 5. F; 6. F; 7. T

Corrected False Statements:

1. Movie titles are often different in different countries.
5. The Taiwanese title for *Deep Impact* was *A Planet Will Hit the Earth.*
6. The Japanese movie *Tampopo* had the same title in the United States.

B. Talk About It

- ❍ Go over the directions and the examples.
- ❍ Put students in pairs to complete the chart. Have students translate two titles and create their own for the other two.
- ❍ Call on students to share their ideas with the class.

ANSWER KEY

Answers will vary.

EXPANSION ACTIVITY: What's in a Name?

- ❍ Put students in pairs to list 10 titles of existing movies that they think are effective.
- ❍ Ask students to identify the characteristics of the titles they have chosen which help sell or advertise the movie.
- ❍ Call on students to share their ideas with the class.

PART 2 GENERAL INTEREST READING ADVERTISING THROUGH HISTORY, PAGES 86–91

Before Reading

A. Thinking Ahead

- ❍ Direct students' attention to the photos on page 86.
- ❍ Go over the directions.
- ❍ Put students in small groups to answer the questions.
- ❍ Call on students to share their ideas with the class.

ANSWER KEY

Answers will vary.

Culture Note:

- You may want to point out that the movie advertised on the billboard is a Harry Potter movie, based on the very popular Harry Potter fantasy novels by J. K. Rowling about a boy who is a wizard.

B. Vocabulary Preparation

- Go over the directions. Have students look at the definitions. Explain unfamiliar terms if necessary.
- Have students match the rest of the definitions to the words in color by writing the letters on the lines next to the sentences.
- Have students check their answers with a partner.
- Go over the answers with the class.

ANSWER KEY

1. e; 2. h; 3. d; 4. c; 5. f; 6. g; 7. a; 8. b

EXPANSION ACTIVITY: Word Scrambles

- Give students one minute to review the new vocabulary words. Have students close their books.
- Tell students you will dictate a series of letters which they will then unscramble to write one of the new vocabulary words.
- Create scrambles for the words like the following:
  i-g-n-r-t-i-t-r-i-a, (irritating)
  t-c-e-l-r-f-e (reflect)
  f-e-v-i-e-f-c-t-e (effective)
- Dictate the scrambled words to the students and have them unscramble the words.

READING STRATEGY: Guessing the Meaning of New Words: Adjective Clauses with *Who* and *That*

- Go over the information in the box. Ask: *What does an adjective clause do? What words do adjective clauses begin with?*

Grammar Notes:

- Your students may know that adjective clauses can begin with other relative pronouns (*which, where, when*) or no pronoun at all, but the focus of this chapter will be on those that begin with *who* and *that* only.
- You may want to point out that like adjectives, adjective clauses often tell us which one or what kind. For example, in answer to the question, "What kind of advertisements are commercials?" we can answer, "The kind that are on TV or radio."
- Although there are examples of relative pronouns in both the subject and object positions in the reading, students should be able to understand the meanings.

C. Guessing the Meanings of New Words: Adjective Clauses with *Who* and *That*

- Go over the directions. Encourage students to underline adjective clauses with *who* and *that* in the reading.

Reading

- Go over the directions and the question.
- Have students read the passage silently, or play the audio program as students follow along.
- After students have finished reading, elicit ideas about how advertising in the past is similar to advertising today.

After Reading

A. Main Idea

- Go over the directions. Have students fill in the bubble next to the main idea. Encourage them to review the reading if necessary.
- Go over the answer with the class.

ANSWER KEY
B

READING STRATEGY: Making Notes
❍ Go over the information in the box. Ask comprehension questions such as: *What are some things you should underline or circle as you read?*

TOEFL® iBT Tip

TOEFL iBT TIP 1: The TOEFL iBT permits examinees to take notes in both the reading and listening sections of the test, and apply those notes to the discrete items tested in those sections as well as in the integrated part of the test.

❍ Point out that the strategy, *Making Notes,* will help students keep information organized and identify key words in a text on the TOEFL iBT.

❍ In the integrated writing section of the test, students are encouraged to refer to information from the text or lecture. Excellent note taking will help students improve their overall reading, writing, and listening skills for the test.

B. Finding Details
❍ Go over the directions and have students reread the passage to underline or circle the information.
❍ Have students match the type of advertising with the correct times and places and then check their answers with a partner.
❍ Go over the answers with the class.

ANSWER KEY
1. d; 2. a; 3. c; 4. b;

C. Vocabulary Check
❍ Go over the directions and the example.
❍ Have students complete the sentences with words or phrases from the box and then check their answers with a partner.
❍ Go over the answers with the class.

ANSWER KEY
1. values; 2. packaging; 3. town criers; 4. trademark; 5. Outdoor displays

EXPANSION ACTIVITY: Advertising Jeopardy
❍ Divide the class into teams. Give students five minutes to study the reading.
❍ Write the following headings on the board: *Places, Times, Products/Inventions, Other Ad Facts.* Under each heading, write the following point values: 100, 200, 300, 400, 500.
❍ Explain the game: Teams will take turns. On their turn, a team will choose a category and a point value. The question for that point value will then be read. If they answer the question correctly, they will earn the designated number of points. If they answer incorrectly, those points will be deducted from their score. A different team member should answer each question on each turn, although team members can assist. Set a time limit of 30 seconds.
❍ Call on the first team and ask the question they select. Award points as appropriate. Continue alternating teams until all the questions have been asked.

Places
100 - Where were hikifuda used? (*Japan*)
200 - What country first used print ads? (*China*)
300 - Where were town criers popular? (*Europe*)
400 - Where were the first billboards found? (*Rome*)
500 - Where are the pictures located on hikifuda? (*on the right*)

Times
100 - During what time period did Internet movies become popular? (*early 2000s, now*)
200 - When were hikifuda used? (*late 1800s*)
300 - When were town criers popular? (*500–1500 A.D.*)
400 - When did the first billboards exist? (*more than 2,000 years ago*)

500 - During what time frame did the first package ads appear? (*1271–1368 A.D.*)

Products/Inventions

100 - What product was advertised using an Internet movie? (*BMW car*)

200 - The first printed ads were for what product? (*paint*)

300 - What type of advertising sold products using values such as luck and prosperity? (*hikifuda*)

400 - What invention changed advertising in Europe in the 1400s? (*printing press*)

500 - What two things were invented first in China? (*paper, printing*)

Other Ad Facts

100 - How old are the oldest ads? (*over 5,000 years*)

200 - How are hikifuda made? (*with woodblocks*)

300 - Which ad mentioned in the reading first featured a trademark? (*print ad for paint*)

400 - Who is the actor in the Internet ad mentioned in the reading? (*Clive Owen*)

500 - Who is the market for the BMW Z4 roadster? (*males with incomes of $75,000 or higher*)

D. Application

- ❍ Go over the directions. Direct students' attention to the ads and ask questions: *What do you see? What are the products?*
- ❍ Put students in small groups to discuss the questions.
- ❍ Call on students to share their ideas with the class.

ANSWER KEY

1. The ads include the names of the manufacturer and a picture of the product.
2. Tag Heuer and Sony Playstation use logos. The Tag Heuer logo looks like a five-sided badge. The Sony Playstation logo is made up of the letters S and P.
3. Answers may vary. Ideas might include the following: Tag Heuer watches reflect boldness, first class. Sony Playstation reflects power.
4. Answers may vary. Ideas might include the following: In the watch ad, the advertisers use a famous person (Tiger Woods) and a large watch to get attention. The Sony ad uses a mysterious face and extended hand.

CRITICAL THINKING STRATEGY: Evaluation

- ❍ Point out that when we evaluate something, we are making a judgment about it according to certain criteria. For example, we may judge a movie to be good if it is exciting and has good acting. The criteria for evaluating the movie would be the level of excitement and the quality of the acting. The criteria will differ according to what we are judging.
- ❍ The following expansion activity, *Evaluating Practice*, can be used for practice in evaluating ads.

EXPANSION ACTIVITY: Evaluating Practice

- ❍ Direct students' attention to the ads in Activity D. Ask: *Which ads do you think are successful? Why? What are your criteria?*
- ❍ Bring in ads from magazines or newspapers, or have students bring in ads.
- ❍ Collect the ads and sort them, putting ads for similar products together.
- ❍ Put students in pairs or small groups. Give each pair or small group several ads that promote similar products.
- ❍ Have students compare the ads. Ask students to choose criteria for evaluation and write them down.
- ❍ Ask students to evaluate the ads according to the criteria they chose and rank each ad according to its effectiveness.
- ❍ Have each pair or small group share their criteria and evaluations with the class.

PART 3 ACADEMIC READING MODERN ADVERTISING, PAGES 92–98

Before Reading

A. Thinking Ahead

- Direct students' attention to the photos. Ask: *What are they advertising? Do you use any of these products?*
- Go over the directions.
- Put students in small groups to discuss the question.
- Go over student ideas with the class.

ANSWER KEY

Answers will vary.

Culture Note:

- You may want to discuss with your students differences in values in different countries. For example, in the United States, ads often promote the values seen in these ads of youth, luxury, and energy.

EXPANSION ACTIVITY: Compare and Contrast

- Put students in small groups and assign each group a country.
- For an out-of-class assignment, have students collect magazine ads from two different countries (their own and the assigned country). Suggest students visit libraries, newspaper stands, or online sources to get copies of the ads. You may want to bring in the ads if students have difficulty accessing these resources.
- Have students list the values they see depicted in the ads from the two countries.
- Call on representatives from each group to present to the class the group's findings.

B. Vocabulary Preparation

- Go over the directions and the example.
- Have students match the definitions with the words and then compare their ideas with a partner.
- Go over the answers with the class.

ANSWER KEY

1. g; 2. c; 3. a; 4. e; 5. h; 6. b; 7. d; 8. f

READING STRATEGY: Guessing the Meanings of New Words: Colons

- Go over the information in the box. Make sure students understand that examples as well as definitions may follow colons.
- Point out that colons used to give an example or explanation are often used near the end of the sentence.

EXPANSION ACTIVITY: Do It Yourself

- Have students choose three vocabulary words from Activity B and write original sentences, using colons to help explain the meanings of the words.
- Put students in pairs to read their sentences.
- Call on students to share their sentences with the class.

C. Guessing the Meanings of New Words: Colons

- Go over the directions.
- Have students scan the reading to notice the use of colons. Elicit examples of explanations following colons.

TOEFL® iBT Tip

TOEFL iBT TIP 2: The TOEFL iBT tests the ability to determine the meaning of words in context.

❍ Point out that the strategy, *Guessing the Meanings of New Words: Colons,* will help students improve their vocabulary for the TOEFL iBT. By identifying words that are used as examples or explanations of other words and understanding their meanings, students will be able to apply this information toward further understanding the concepts presented in the text.

❍ Useful vocabulary words or terms from the reading include the following: *luxurious lifestyle, different methods, name brands, and grafitti.*

On the TOEFL iBT this question appears in the following format:

The word ______ in the passage is closest in meaning to …

Reading

❍ Go over the directions and the question.
❍ Have students read the passage silently, or play the audio program and have students follow along silently.
❍ Elicit examples of how advertisers reach consumers.

Culture Notes:

❍ SUVs, or sports utility vehicles, are very popular in the United States.
❍ *Men in Black* (1997) is a popular movie about aliens. The poster shows the sequel, *Men in Black II* (2002).
❍ *Cast Away* (2000) is a movie about a man who is stranded alone on an island for a long time. During his time on the island, he creates a friend by using a Wilson brand volleyball that had washed ashore.
❍ *ET* (1982) is a movie about an extra-terrestrial who becomes friends with a little boy named Elliot. They eat the peanut-butter candy Reese's Pieces.
❍ *Crazy Taxi* is a video game in which the player takes on the role of a taxi driver and tries to earn a lot of money.
❍ Pizza Hut is an American chain of restaurants that sells mostly pizza.
❍ Pepsi is a cola soft drink.
❍ *Mission Impossible* (1996) is a movie based on a popular TV show from the 1960s–1970s about secret intelligence agents.
❍ Powerbooks are laptop computers made by Apple. Apple is the primary alternative to the personal computers made by IBM, Dell, and others. It uses a different operating system from Microsoft Windows.

After Reading

A. Check Your Understanding

❍ Go over the directions.
❍ Have students fill in *T* or *F* for each statement and then check their answers with a partner.
❍ Go over the answers with the class.

ANSWER KEY

1. T; 2. F; 3. T; 4. F; 5. F

READING STRATEGY: Finding Examples

❍ Go over the information in the box. Ask: *What words do examples often follow?*

 B. Practice: Finding Examples

❍ Go over the directions.
❍ Direct students' attention to the examples in the box. Have students find the examples in the reading and underline them.
❍ Have students write the letter of the example next to each sentence.
❍ Put students in pairs to compare answers.
❍ Go over the answers with the class.

ANSWER KEY

1. c; 2. b; 3. a

TOEFL® iBT Tip

TOEFL iBT TIP 3: The TOEFL iBT measures the ability to understand key facts and important information in a passage. This type of question is a factual information question.

- Remind students that the strategy and activity for *Finding Examples* will help them understand main points in a reading and apply them to various question types.

- Interpreting information in this way may also help with the schematic table and categorizing question types.

On the TOEFL iBT this question may appear in the following format:

According to the passage/paragraph ___, …

EXPANSION ACTIVITY: Organizing Information

- Photocopy the Black Line Master *Organizing Information* on page BLM 6 and distribute it to students.
- Explain that mapping is another way to organize information graphically. Tell students that when we map or cluster ideas, we usually write the main idea or topic in a circle in the middle of the page. Other main ideas are presented in outlying circles. Examples and details are then presented in circles around the main ideas.
- Go over the example cluster on the worksheet.
- Have students complete the map, and then compare ideas with a partner. Have students add circles for other connected ideas as needed.
- Copy the graphic organizer on the board, and ask for volunteers to fill in the circles with their ideas.

C. Vocabulary Check

- Go over the directions.
- Have students complete the sentences with words and phrases from the box.
- Go over the answers with the class.

ANSWER KEY

1. image; 2. personalize; 3. qualities; 4. fact of life; 5. name brands

READING STRATEGY: Recognizing Word Forms

- Go over the information in the box. Ask: *What endings often indicate a noun? What ending indicates an adjective?*

D. Practice: Recognizing Word Forms

- Go over the directions.
- Have students complete the chart and then compare charts with a partner.
- Go over the answers with the class.

ANSWER KEY

Verb	Noun (thing)	Noun (person)	Adjective
advertise	advertisement	advertiser	
consume		consumer	
	fame		famous
	luxury		luxurious
place	placement		
write		writer	

TOEFL® iBT Tip

TOEFL iBT TIP 4: The TOEFL iBT tests the ability to understand key words and vocabulary contained within a text.

- Point out that being able to recognize word forms will help students improve their overall vocabulary.

- TOEFL iBT reading passages (and lectures) will incorporate words that may be derived from words that students are familiar with, but also forms that may not be as common.

- Activity D, *Practice: Recognizing Word Forms,* is also helpful for students to practice and prepare for the schematic chart question type, which requires higher critical thinking skills.

CRITICAL THINKING STRATEGY: Synthesizing

- Remind students that when they put together information from different sources, they are synthesizing (as in Activity E).

E. Making Connections: Parts 2 and 3

- Go over the directions.
- Put students in small groups to discuss the commercial.
- Call on students to share their ideas with the class.

ANSWER KEY

Answers may vary but might include the following: The commercial might have appealed to the need to feel good about themselves and better than others. The product image was one of luxury and power.

F. Journal Writing

- Go over the directions.
- Explain that this is a quick-writing activity and does not have to be perfect. Point out that journal writing can be a warm-up to a more structured writing assignment, helping to generate ideas.
- Have students write. Set a time limit of five minutes.
- Put students in pairs to read or talk about their writing.

Website Research

- For additional information on advertising, you could direct students to:
  - Advertising & Material Culture History, The Media History Project (http://www.mediahistory.umn.edu/advert.html)
  - Advertising, Marketing and Commercial Imagery Collections, National Museum of American History (http://americanhistory.si.edu/archives/d-7.htm)
  - Internet Advertising History—EC2@USC (http://www.ec2.edu/dccenter/archives/ia/history.html)
  - Common Advertising Strategies—Media Awareness Network (http://www.media-awareness.ca/english/resources/educational/handouts/advertising_marketing/common_ad_strats.cfm)

PART 4 THE MECHANICS OF WRITING, PAGES 99–102

- Go over the directions.

The Present Continuous Tense

- Go over the information in the box about the present continuous tense. Ask: *When do we use the present continuous? How many parts does the verb have?*

A. Practice: Spelling

- Review the spelling rules on page 168.
- Go over the directions.
- Have students write the *–ing* form of each verb.
- Put students in pairs to check their answers.
- Call on volunteers to write the words on the board or spell them out loud to the class.

ANSWER KEY

1. sharing; 2. doing; 3. solving; 4. admiring; 5. advertising; 6. making; 7. studying; 8. selling

B. Practice: The Present Continuous Tense

- Go over the directions.
- Have students fill in the blanks with the correct forms of the verbs in parentheses.
- Have students check their answers with a partner.
- Go over the answers with the class.

ANSWER KEY

1. are driving; 2. is admiring; 3. are talking; are smiling; 4. are wearing; 5. is sitting; is studying

EXPANSION ACTIVITY: Apply It

❍ Direct students' attention to the ads in Part 3 of this chapter (page 92 in the student book).
❍ Have students write a sentence using the present continuous about each ad.
❍ Put students in pairs to compare sentences.
❍ Call on students to share their ideas with the class.

ANSWER KEY

Answers may vary but might include the following:
The people in the ad are smiling.
The woman is sitting.
The man is ski-boarding.
The woman is waiting.

Review: The Simple Present Tense/ Subject-Verb Agreement

❍ Go over the information in the boxes.
❍ Ask: *When do we use the simple present? What are some examples of words that are singular but refer to more than one thing?*

C. Practice: Subject-Verb Agreement

❍ Go over the directions.
❍ Have students fill in the blanks with the correct forms of the verbs in parentheses.
❍ Have students check their answers with a partner.
❍ Go over the answers with the class.

ANSWER KEY

are; is; sees; says; turns; notices; seems; open; jumps

Showing Order

❍ Go over the information in the box. Point out that these words are similar in function to the adverbial conjunctions students practiced in Chapter 3 *(first, second, third).*

D. Practice: Showing Order

❍ Go over the directions.
❍ Read Event 1 and elicit a sentence with an order word *(First, the boy starts running.).*
❍ Have students write the sentences in a paragraph using order words.
❍ Have students compare their paragraphs with a partner.
❍ Call on students to read their paragraphs to the class.

ANSWER KEY

Answers will vary though the event order should remain the same.

EXPANSION ACTIVITY: Describe a Process

❍ Model the activity by describing a process you know well *(I make coffee every morning. First, I fill a pot with water and put it on the stove to boil. Then …).*
❍ Give students two minutes to choose a process and make some notes.
❍ Put students in pairs to take turns describing the process.
❍ Call on students to describe the process to the class.

Adjectives

❍ Go over the information in the box.
❍ Ask: *Where do adjectives often go in the sentence? What verbs often go before an adjective?*

Vocabulary Note:

❍ Your students may have already noticed in this chapter that some adjectives end in *–ous*. You may want to point out or elicit other common endings for adjectives *(–y, –ive, –al).*

E. Practice: Adjectives

❍ Go over the directions and the example.
❍ Put students in pairs to write five sentences about commercials.
❍ Call on students to read sentences to the class.

ANSWER KEY

Answers will vary.

EXPANSION ACTIVITY: Category Beanbag Toss

- Brainstorm a list of categories of adjectives and write them on the board *(colors, shapes, sizes, materials, quality, nationalities).*
- Elicit an example for each category.
- Call on a student and toss a ball or beanbag as you say a category *(color)*. The student should give an example of that type of adjective when they catch the ball or beanbag *(red)*.
- Direct the student to toss the ball or beanbag to another student and say a different category.
- Continue until everyone has had a chance to participate.

Adverbs

- Go over the information in the box.
- Ask: *What ending do we add to adjectives to form adverbs? What do adverbs do? Where do we sometimes put adverbs?*

Grammar Notes:

- You may want to point out that usually when we put an adverb first, the adverb describes the entire sentence, not just the verb.
- When the adverb describes the verb only, it often goes next to the verb or even between verb parts *(I have almost finished the job; She walked quickly to the store.).*

F. Practice: Adverbs

- Go over the directions.
- Have students complete the sentences with the adverb form of the words in parentheses and then check their answers with a partner.
- Go over the answers with the class.

ANSWER KEY

1. perfectly; 2. quietly; 3. neatly; 4. quickly; 5. differently

Words in Phrases: *It Is, There Is/Are*

- Go over the information in the box.
- Ask: *What expression do we use to describe weather? What do we use to describe people or objects in a scene? How do you know when to use* there is *and when to use* there are?

G. Practice: Words in Phrases

- Go over the directions and the example.
- Put students in small groups to discuss the ads.
- Remind students to use *it is* and *there is/are* in their discussions.
- Call on students to share their ideas with the class.

ANSWER KEY

Answers will vary.

H. Review: Editing a Paragraph

- Go over the directions.
- Have students find and correct the seven mistakes. Have students check their answers with a partner.
- Go over the answers with the class.

ANSWER KEY

In this commercial, you see a small puppy. At the beginning, he is lying on the kitchen floor. He seems tired. There's a big bowl of food near him, but he doesn't eat it. He looks sad. Then, a woman comes into the kitchen. She calls the puppy, but he doesn't come. He just lies there. Next, she gives him a new kind of puppy food. The puppy tries the food. He eats it loudly. Suddenly, the dog has energy. He looks happy and alive. He runs across the room and jumps into the woman's arms.

TOEFL® iBT Tip

TOEFL iBT TIP 5: Although the TOEFL iBT does not discretely test grammar skills, examinees' essay scores will be determined based on the range of grammar and vocabulary used in their essays.

- ❍ Point out that the grammar activities in *The Mechanics of Writing* part of this chapter will help them improve their abilities to write descriptive essays, using adverbs, adjectives, *there is/there are,* and editing their essays for subject-verb agreement and word order.

PART 5 ACADEMIC WRITING, PAGES 103–107

Writing Assignment

- ❍ Go over the directions.

Model

- ❍ Have students read the six steps of the example.
- ❍ Direct students' attention to Step A of the example, and ask: *What topic did the student choose?*
- ❍ Direct students' attention to Step B. Ask: *What questions did the student use to get ideas?* Elicit other ways to gather ideas.
- ❍ Direct students' attention to Step C. Elicit examples of when the student used *it is* or *there is/are*. Ask students if they notice any mistakes.
- ❍ Have students read the paragraph in Step D of the example and notice when the writer used words to show order and adverbs.
- ❍ Direct students' attention to Step E. Ask: *How many mistakes did the writer circle in the paragraph in Step D? What are they?*
- ❍ Have students read the paragraph in Step F. Ask: *How did the writer correct the mistakes?*

Your Turn

- ❍ Have students read Step A and choose a topic.
- ❍ Have students answer the questions in Step B. You may want to put students in pairs to discuss their ideas.
- ❍ Have students complete Step C.

WRITING STRATEGY: Writing a Paragraph

- ❍ Go over the information in the box. Ask questions: *Where do we often express the main idea of a paragraph? What do the other sentences do? How can we connect the ideas in the sentences?*

(**Your Turn**, *continued*)

- ❍ Have students follow Step D. and copy their sentences from Step C. Encourage students to use words showing order to connect the ideas.
- ❍ If you want to have students practice peer editing skills, have them exchange paragraphs with a partner and comment on mistakes or other problems.
- ❍ Ask students to edit their paragraphs (Step E) and then rewrite (Step F).
- ❍ Collect the paragraphs.

EXPANSION ACTIVITY: Connect Ideas

- ❍ Distribute seven or eight index cards to each student and have students write each sentence from their paragraphs on a separate card. Or, have students write their sentences on a piece of paper, skipping a line between each sentence, then cut the sentences into strips.
- ❍ Have students shuffle their cards or strips.
- ❍ Put students in pairs to exchange sets of cards or strips. Have students recreate their partner's paragraph by putting the sentences in correct order and then check with their partner.
- ❍ Repeat the activity with new partners.

TOEFL® iBT Tip

TOEFL iBT TIP 6: Both the integrated and independent essays of the TOEFL iBT will be scored based on how well the examinee completes the overall writing task.

❍ Point out that the paragraph writing activities in *The Academic Writing* part of this chapter will help students improve their coherence and ability to link the flow of ideas in their essays by taking smaller steps in their essay development.

❍ Remind students that working slowly with sentence by sentence combination will help them develop their paragraphs more concisely, and likely improve their overall essay scores.

Unit 2 Vocabulary Workshop

- Have students review vocabulary from Chapters 3 and 4.

A. Matching

- Go over the directions.
- Have students write the correct letters on the lines to match the definitions with the words.
- Go over the answers.

ANSWER KEY

1. e; 2. i; 3. h; 4. b; 5. a; 6. c; 7. d; 8. f; 9. j; 10. g

B. Sentence Halves

- Go over the directions.
- Have students match the first halves of the sentences with the correct second halves.
- Go over the answers.

ANSWER KEY

1. d; 2. e; 3. f; 4. a; 5. b; 6. c

C. Words in Phrases: Prepositions

- Go over the directions.
- Have students write the words from the box on the lines. Note that students will use some prepositions more than once.
- Go over the answers.

ANSWER KEY

1. in; 2. about; 3. in; 4. of; 5. to; 6. of; 7. to; 8. in

D. Which Word Doesn't Belong?

- Go over the directions.
- Have students cross out the word that doesn't belong for each row.
- Have students check their answers.
- Go over the answers.

ANSWER KEY

1. admire; 2. highlights; 3. strength; 4. talent; 5. discovery; 6. image; 7. logos; 8. irritating

UNIT 3

Unit Opener, page 111

- ❍ Direct students' attention to the photo and unit and chapter titles on page 111. Ask questions: *What do you think the unit will be about? What do you know about this topic?*
- ❍ Brainstorm ideas for what the unit will include and write students' ideas on the board.

CHAPTER 5 PARENTING, GENDER, AND STEREOTYPES

In this chapter, students will read about parenting, gender, and stereotypes. In the first reading, students will read about Jane Goodall, a British researcher, and her study of chimpanzee society in the wilds of Africa and similarities to human society. In the second reading, students will look more closely at how toys affect the socialization and gender stereotyping of children, especially how toys influence language and conversation development. In the last reading, students will learn about research into how stereotyping of all types can affect people. These topics will prepare students to write about an important lesson they learned from playing as children.

VOCABULARY

adulthood	eye contact	prepare	siblings	vocal
amount	general	questionnaire	sociologists	worse
briefly	grocery store	races	son	
choice	imagine	relationships	stereotypes	
daughter	infants	researchers	tasks	
elderly	mature	results	take apart	

READING STRATEGIES

Guessing the Meanings of New Words: *In Other Words*
Infinitives of Purpose
Understanding the Word *So*
Previewing a Reading
Guessing the Meanings of New Words: *That Is*
Finding the Main Idea: Using Topic Sentences

CRITICAL THINKING STRATEGIES

Comparing and Contrasting (Part 1)
Understanding Cause and Effect (Part 2)
Making Inferences (Part 3)
Note: The strategy in bold is highlighted in the Student Book.

MECHANICS

Using the Word *When*
Using the Word *So*
Review: Conjunctions
Using the Phrase *Used To*
Finding Words in Phrases

WRITING STRATEGY

Editing Your Paragraph

CHAPTER 5 Parenting, Gender, and Stereotypes

Chapter 5 Opener, page 113

- ❍ Direct students' attention to the photo. Ask them what is happening in the photo.
- ❍ Have students discuss the four questions. This can be done in pairs, in small groups, or as a class.
- ❍ Check students' predictions of the chapter topic.

PART 1 INTRODUCTION PARENTING IN CHIMP SOCIETY, PAGES 114–116

Before Reading

Thinking Ahead

- ❍ Have students look at the photos.
- ❍ Put students in pairs to answer the questions.
- ❍ Call on students to share their ideas with the class.

ANSWER KEY

Answers will vary.

Reading

- ❍ Have students look at the reading. Ask: *What is this story about? (parenting in chimp society).* Go over the directions and the question.
- ❍ Have students read the passage silently, or have students follow along silently as you play the audio program.
- ❍ Ask students how chimpanzee society is similar to human society.

EXPANSION ACTIVITY: Group Notes

- ❍ Write the headings for this reading on large sheets of paper: *Parenting in Chimp Society, Introduction to the Chimps of Gombe, Chimps: Social Primates, Learning.* Tape the sheets of paper around the classroom.
- ❍ Divide the class into four groups.
- ❍ Explain the activity: Every student will write at least one word related to the heading on the paper on each sheet, either something they remember from the reading or something the reading reminds them of.
- ❍ Have each group move to one of the sheets of paper. Set a time limit of one to two minutes, reminding students that everyone needs to write something. Encourage students to add something new to the notes.
- ❍ Call time, and have the groups rotate to a new sheet of paper and continue.
- ❍ For large classes, you may want to put students into groups of four. Within each group, students can circulate sheets of paper for each heading in the reading. If you choose this variation, you need to have students rotate sheets every 10–15 seconds, but you can allow students to circulate the sheets more than once.
- ❍ When the activity is completed, discuss the kind of information the students added to the sheets.

After Reading

A. Check Your Understanding

- ❍ Go over the directions.
- ❍ Have students fill in *T* or *F* next to each sentence.
- ❍ Have students check their answers with a partner.
- ❍ Go over the answers with the class. For additional practice, have students correct the false statements.

ANSWER KEY

1. T; 2. T; 3. T; 4. F; 5. F

Corrected False Statements:

4. Chimps and humans use tools.
5. Chimps learn from other chimps, just like humans learn from other humans.

EXPANSION ACTIVITY: True/False Chain

- ❍ Have students write five to ten additional true or false statements based on the reading.
- ❍ Give students five minutes to review the reading.
- ❍ Have students stand in a line or circle. Start the activity: say a statement about the reading to the student at the end of the line. Elicit whether the statement is true or false. If it is false, elicit the correct statement from the student.
- ❍ Have that student say or read one of their written statements to the student standing to their right. The student on the right will say if the statement is true or false and correct if necessary.
- ❍ Continue until everyone has participated.

B. Talk About It

- ❍ Go over the directions.
- ❍ Put students in small groups to answer the questions.
- ❍ Call on students to share their ideas with the class.

ANSWER KEY

1. Answers may vary. Ideas might include the following: live in groups, close to mother and siblings, some female chimps are better mothers, learn through play and observing others, can use tools.
2. Answers will vary.

CRITICAL THINKING STRATEGY: Comparing and Contrasting

- ❍ Comparing and contrasting are ways to analyze what we know about a topic, and so better understand it.
- ❍ Point out that Activity B and the following Venn diagram expansion activity allow students to compare and contrast chimps and humans.

EXPANSION ACTIVITY: Venn Diagrams

- ❍ Review how to draw a Venn diagram. Draw one on the board, with *chimps* in one circle, *humans* in the other, and *both* in the middle.
- ❍ Have students create Venn diagrams to compare and contrast chimps and humans.
- ❍ Put students in pairs to compare diagrams.
- ❍ Elicit ideas and complete the diagram on the board.

PART 2 GENERAL INTEREST READING

CHILDREN, GENDER, AND TOYS, PAGES 117–123

Before Reading

A. Thinking Ahead

- ❍ Go over the directions.
- ❍ Have students stand and move around and ask classmates for their opinions. Remind students to tally the answers in the appropriate columns. Students should try to ask at least five students for their opinions.
- ❍ Call on students to tell the class about their findings.

ANSWER KEY

Answers will vary.

EXPANSION ACTIVITY: Bar Graphs

- ❍ Explain that bar charts or graphs are a good way to visually present the results of a survey or questionnaire.
- ❍ Model the activity. Use questions from the *Thinking Ahead* questionnaire *(Who is better at math in school?)*, and have students raise their hands to indicate their answers *(Raise your hand if you think boys are better; Raise your hand if you think girls are better; Raise your hand if you think neither are better than the other at math.)*. Tally the results and write the total for each on the board *(Boys 9, Girls 6, Neither 8)*.

❍ Create a bar graph like the example below to represent the results.

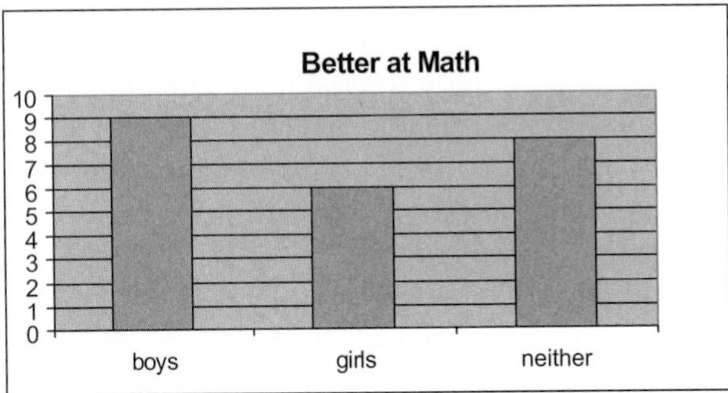

❍ Have students create bar graphs to present the results for two of the questions that their classmates answered in the *Thinking Ahead* questionnaire.

❍ Put students in pairs to talk about their graphs.

B. Vocabulary Preparation

❍ Go over the directions. Have students look at the definitions. Explain unfamiliar terms if necessary.

❍ If your students need more help with pronunciation, read the definitions aloud and have students repeat, then read the sentences aloud and have students repeat.

❍ Go over the example.

❍ Have students match the rest of the definitions to the words in blue by writing the letters on the lines next to the sentences.

❍ Have students check their answers with a partner.

❍ Go over the answers with the class.

ANSWER KEY

1. f; 2. e; 3. b; 4. d; 5. g; 6. c; 7. h; 8. a

READING STRATEGY: Guessing the Meanings of New Words: *In Other Words*

❍ Go over the information in the box.

EXPANSION ACTIVITY: In Other Words

❍ Have students choose three vocabulary words from Activity B.

❍ Have students write sentences explaining the three words using *in other words.*

❍ Put students in pairs to read their sentences aloud.

❍ Call on students to read their sentences to the class.

C. Guessing the Meanings of New Words: *In Other Words*

❍ Go over the directions.

TOEFL® iBT Tip

TOEFL iBT TIP 1: The TOEFL iBT tests the ability to determine the meanings of words in context.

❍ Point out that the strategy, *Guessing the Meanings of New Words: In Other Words,* will help students improve their vocabulary for the TOEFL iBT. Not only will understanding how to use the phrase *in other words* help students understand meaning, it will also be useful as a technique for summarizing and paraphrasing a reading and applying it to essay writing.

Academic Note:

❍ You may want to point out that we learn and remember more about new information when it builds on what we already know. Elicit from students what they know about nature vs. nurture from Chapter 1. This will help students activate background knowledge.

Reading

❍ Go over the directions and the questions.

❍ Have students read the passage silently, or play the audio program and have students follow along silently. If you choose to do the expansion activity below, give students a couple of minutes to read each section, and then stop for discussion.

EXPANSION ACTIVITY: Stop and Discuss

❍ Remind students that they can often learn more from a reading if they make connections to their own experiences.

❍ Write the following on the board.

- *Children, Gender, and Toys: Are the generalizations about boys and girls true in your experience?*
- *The Influence of Nature: Have you seen parents interact differently with their daughters and sons?*

- *The Influence of Toys: What were your favorite toys and games when you were very young?*
- *The Influence of Parents: What kinds of toys did your parents buy you?*

❍ Set a time limit for reading each section that is appropriate for your students. When students have read the section, put students in pairs to answer the question for that section.

After Reading

A. Check Your Understanding

❍ Go over the directions.
❍ Have students check the true statements.
❍ Go over the answers with the class.

ANSWER KEY

Check: 1, 3, 4, 5

B. Finding Details

❍ Go over the directions.
❍ Have students complete the graphic organizer and then compare ideas with a partner.
❍ Go over the answers with the class.

ANSWER KEY

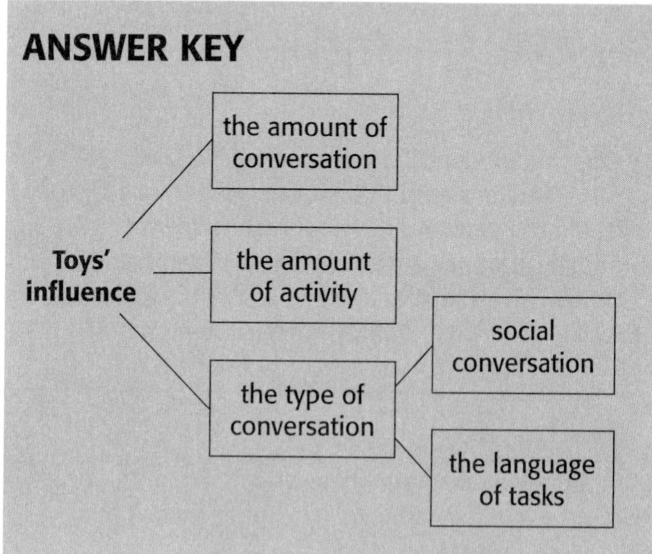

TOEFL® iBT Tip

TOEFL iBT TIP 2: The TOEFL iBT does not directly test the ability to determine the main idea in a text. Instead, examinees may be required to distinguish between major and minor points of information, or create a mental framework for organizing major points and important details.

❍ Point out that the strategy for Activity B, *Finding Details* will help students distinguish between major and minor points in a text on the TOEFL iBT.

❍ Explain to students that this type of question is called a *prose summary* or *classification* question, and partial credit will be given for correct answers. On the TOEFL iBT, the answers to this type of question are not in traditional multiple-choice format.

The question type appears in the form of a schematic table that requires examinees to select and drag answer choices to specific positions in a chart. Partial credit is used for scoring this type of question.

C. Vocabulary Check

❍ Direct students' attention to the words in the box. Say each word and have students repeat.
❍ Go over the directions and the example.
❍ Have students complete the sentences and then check their answers with a partner.
❍ Go over the answers with the class.

ANSWER KEY

1. eye contact; 2. vocal; 3. grocery store; 4. amount; 5. tasks; 6. relationships

D. Vocabulary Extension: Words with *–hood*

❍ Go over the directions.
❍ Have students write the words next to the definitions.
❍ Go over the answers.

ANSWER KEY

1. childhood; 2. parenthood; 3. motherhood; 4. fatherhood

READING STRATEGY: Infinitives of Purpose

- Go over the information in the box. Ask: *How do we form the infinitive? What question does an infinitive of purpose answer?*

E. Practice: Infinitives of Purpose

- Go over the directions.
- Have students answer the questions.
- Go over the answers.

ANSWER KEY

1. Parents might buy a "girl's toy" for their son to help him prepare for future relationships.
2. They might buy a "boy's toy" for their daughter to help her prepare for a future career.

READING STRATEGY: Understanding the Word *So*

- Go over the information in the box. Ask: *What is one meaning of the word* so?

CRITICAL THINKING STRATEGY: Understanding Cause and Effect

- Understanding cause and effect is an important critical thinking strategy. One word that signals this relationship is *so.* Other words include *because, therefore, because of, due to.*

F. Practice: Understanding the Word *So*

- Go over the directions.
- Have students answer the questions. Remind them to use the word *so* in their answers.
- Put students in pairs to compare answers.
- Go over the answers with the class.

Grammar Note:

- Your students may have learned some other uses for *so.* One meaning of *so* is almost the opposite of the meaning expressed in this strategy. When we say *I arrived early so I could get a good seat,* we are using *so* to express a purpose rather than a reason. We use *so that* to express this meaning also.
- Another meaning for *so* is to indicate degree, as in *I love you so much.*

ANSWER KEY

1. Girls usually play with toys such as toy grocery stores, so they practice more language than boys do.
2. Boys usually play with toys like toy cars, so they practice doing things such as problem solving.

G. Application

- Have students discuss the questions in small groups.
- Call on students to share ideas with the class.

ANSWER KEY

Answers will vary.

EXPANSION ACTIVITY: Inside Outside Circles

- Model the activity with a student. Call on a student and ask a *why* question *(Why are you taking this English class?)*. Elicit the answer *(I want a job with an international company.)*. Ask the student to combine the question and answer using *so (I want a job with an international company, so I'm taking this English class.)*.
- Have students think of three *why* questions.
- Ask students to stand and form two concentric circles. The inner circle should face out and the outer circle should face in. Each student should be facing another student.
- Explain the activity: The students on the inside circle will ask a *why* question, which the partners on the outside will answer using *so.* Then students will switch roles. You will then call out "move" and the inside circle will move one person to the right. Everyone should be facing a new partner. Students will repeat with their new partner.
- Begin the activity, reminding students to take turns asking and answering questions. After 30 seconds, have students in the inside circle move to the right.
- Continue for several rotations. Encourage students to ask different questions.

❍ Call on students to tell the class something they learned about another student.

PART 3 ACADEMIC READING STEREOTYPES AND THEIR EFFECTS, PAGES 124–129

Before Reading

READING STRATEGY: Previewing a Reading

❍ Go over the information in the box. Ask: *What is one way to preview a reading?*

Academic Notes:

❍ Although the reading strategy provides information about what to look for when previewing, you may want to cover specifics with your students, including the following:

- Notice formatting: Bold-face, italics, larger font size, and underlining may indicate key ideas in the reading, as well as signal headings and sub-headings.
- Notice visuals: Photos, graphs, cartoons, and diagrams can all provide information about the reading's main ideas and details.
- Skim first and last sentences: In American articles and texts, writers often put the main idea of the paragraph in the first or last sentences. Quickly skimming these sentences can provide a lot of information.

A. Practice: Previewing a Reading

❍ Go over the directions. Make sure students understand how to use headings to get information about the reading.

❍ Have students work in pairs to answer the questions.

❍ Call on students to share their ideas with the class.

ANSWER KEY

Answers will vary. Students should predict that the reading will be about the effects of stereotypes of all kinds (gender, age, race, ethnicity).

B. Vocabulary Preparation

❍ Go over the directions and the example.

❍ Have students match the definitions to the words in blue and then check their answers with a partner.

❍ Go over the answers with the class.

ANSWER KEY

1. b; 2. g; 3. a; 4. e; 5. f; 6. c; 7. d

EXPANSION ACTIVITY: Beanbag Toss

❍ Give students five minutes to review the vocabulary words from this chapter. Write the words on the board. (Words are listed on page 56 of the Teacher's Edition.)

❍ Explain the activity. You will first call on a student and then toss a ball or beanbag to the student as you say a vocabulary word. The student will use the word in a sentence when the student catches the ball or beanbag.

❍ Call on a student and then toss the ball or beanbag as you say one of the vocabulary words *(infant)*. Elicit a sentence from the student *(The infant cried a lot for the first few weeks.)*.

❍ Have the student call on a classmate, toss the ball or beanbag, and say another vocabulary word.

❍ Continue in the same way until everyone has participated.

READING STRATEGY: Guessing the Meanings of New Words: *That Is*

❍ Go over the information in the box.

❍ For extra practice, have students write sentences for vocabulary words from the chapter using *that is* and share with the class.

C. Guessing the Meanings of New Words: *That Is*

- ❍ Go over the directions.
- ❍ Have students highlight or underline definitions that follow *that is* in the reading.

Reading

- ❍ Go over the directions and the questions.
- ❍ Have students read the passage silently, or play the audio program and have students follow along silently.

Culture Notes:

- ❍ You may want to point out to students that the studies described in the reading were conducted in the United States and Canada, and so the results may not necessarily be the same in other countries.
- ❍ In the United States, stereotypes about blacks and whites still exist. Such stereotypes hold that black Americans may be better athletes, while white Americans may be better at intellectual activities.
- ❍ Also, society in the United States is more youth-oriented than in some other cultures. Older people are not always as valued as they are elsewhere.
- ❍ *Newsweek* is a popular news magazine in the United States.

After Reading

READING STRATEGY: Finding the Main Idea: Using Topic Sentences

- ❍ Go over the information in the box. Ask: *What does the topic sentence do? Where can you find a topic sentence?*

A. Practice: Using Topic Sentences

- ❍ Go over the directions.
- ❍ Have students underline or highlight the first sentence in Paragraphs 2–5.

B. Finding the Main Idea

- ❍ Go over the directions.
- ❍ Have students underline the question in the first paragraph and the two sentences that answer the question in the last paragraph.
- ❍ Put students in pairs to check their work.
- ❍ Call on students to share their ideas with the class.

ANSWER KEY

First Paragraph: What is the influence of stereotypes on the targets of those stereotypes?
Last Paragraph: In these studies of people performing mental and physical tasks, all of the research came to the same conclusion: stereotypes of gender, race, ethnic group, and age have an effect on people. Negative stereotypes have a negative effect, so they can be dangerous, but positive stereotypes can have a positive effect.

TOEFL® iBT Tip

TOEFL iBT TIP 3: The TOEFL iBT does not directly test the ability to determine the main idea in a text. Instead, examinees may be required to distinguish between major and minor points of information, or create a mental framework for organizing major points and important details.

- ❍ Point out that the strategy for *Finding the Main Idea* and following activities can help students to find topic sentences that will help them in understanding the overall meaning of the text.
- ❍ This strategy may also help students to recognize logical sequencing of written material. Students will be exposed to the structure of a passage and be able to apply that to essay writing.

C. Vocabulary Check

- ❍ Go over the directions.
- ❍ Have students answer the questions and then compare answers with a partner.
- ❍ Go over the answers with the class.

ANSWER KEY

1. women; 2. Alzheimer's; 3. wise; 4. that they go to a very good university

D. Review: Infinitives of Purpose

❍ Go over the directions.
❍ Have students fill in the chart and then compare charts with a partner.
❍ Go over the answers with the class.

ANSWER KEY

University	Tested	Purpose of the Study
University of Waterloo	math	to test the effects of a gender stereotype
Harvard	math	to see the effects of ethnic and gender stereotypes
Princeton	mini-golf	to nd the effects of racial stereotypes
fiale	memory	to nd the effects of stereotypes of age

EXPANSION ACTIVITY: Inside Outside Circles

❍ In this activity, students will focus on using and answering *why* questions.
❍ Model the activity with a student. Call on a student and ask a *why* question *(Why are you taking this English class?)*. Elicit the answer that uses an infinitive of purpose *(I'm taking this class to get a job with an international company.)*. Have students note this is slightly different than the previous activity that focused on using *so* in the answer.
❍ Have students think of three *why* questions.
❍ Ask students to stand and form two concentric circles. The inner circle should face out and the outer circle face in. Each student should be facing another student.
❍ Explain the activity: The students on the inside circle will ask a *why* question, which the partners on the outside will answer using an infinitive of purpose. Then students will switch roles. You will then call out "move" and the inside circle will move one person to the right. Everyone should be facing a new partner.
❍ Begin the activity, reminding students to take turns asking and answering questions. After 30 seconds, have students in the inside circle move to the right.
❍ Continue for several rotations. Encourage students to ask different questions.
❍ Call on students to tell the class something they learned about another student.

CRITICAL THINKING STRATEGY: Making Inferences

❍ Go over the information in the box. Ask: *What is an inference?*

 E. Practice: Making Inferences

❍ Go over the directions.
❍ Have students answer the questions with information from the reading.
❍ Put students in pairs to share their ideas.
❍ Call on students to share ideas with the class.

ANSWER KEY

1. A positive stereotype of black men is that they have more physical ability. A positive stereotype of white men is that they are better at mental strategies.
2. Group A did worse because of the negative stereotype associated with Alzheimer's. Group B did better because the word "wise" is positive.
3. The stereotype of a Xenrovian is that they are very good at golf, so the question may help him to do better in the golf game.
4. At universities with a bad reputation, being reminded of stereotypes about their school would have a negative effect on students.

TOEFL® iBT Tip

TOEFL iBT TIP 4: The TOEFL iBT tests the ability to make inferences or draw conclusions based on what is implied in a passage.

- Point out that the activity *Making Inferences* requires students to draw conclusions and form generalizations based on information presented in the reading.
- By using key words and phrases from the text, students will be able to apply this skill to the reading section of the TOEFL iBT.

On the TOEFL iBT this question may appear in the following format:

Which of the following can be inferred from paragraph __ about ________ ?

EXPANSION ACTIVITY: Statement to Inference

- Remind students that when we make inferences we use information that is directly stated to make a conclusion that is not directly stated.
- Make a statement *(Lydia was born in the United States and spent her entire life there.)*. Elicit inferences from this statement *(Lydia speaks English; She's an American citizen; She went to school in the United States.)*.
- Ask students to write three statements about themselves.
- Put students in pairs to exchange sentences. Have students write inferences based on each statement.
- Call on students to read one of their partner's sentences and then make an inference about the sentence.

F. Making Connections

- Go over the directions.
- Put students in pairs to answer the questions.
- Call on students to share their ideas with the class.

ANSWER KEY

1. A stereotypical female toy is a toy grocery store. A stereotypical male toy is a toy car.
2. Girls learn the stereotype that girls are good with relationships.
3. Boys learn the stereotype that boys are good with careers.
4. Girls learn the negative stereotype that they don't need to prepare for work.
5. Boys learn the negative stereotype that they don't need to prepare for relationships.

G. Journal Writing

- Go over the directions.
- Explain that this is a quick-writing activity and does not have to be perfect. Point out that journal writing can be a warm-up to a more structured writing assignment, helping to generate ideas.
- Have students write. Set a time limit of five minutes.
- Put students in pairs to read or talk about their writing.

Website Research

- For additional information on stereotype studies, you could direct students to the following websites:
  - Domain Specific Effects of Stereotypes on Performance, Harvard Working Papers (http://ksgnotes1.harvard.edu/Research/wpaper.nsf/rwp/RWP05-026?OpenDocument)
  - Stereotypes Can Reinforce the Status Quo, Stanford Graduate School of Business (http://www.gsb.stanford.edu/news/research/ob_stereotypes.shtml)
  - A Psychological Effect of Stereotypes, by Carrie Conaway (http://www.bos.frb.org/economic/nerr/rr2005/q1/section3c.pdf)
  - Racial Stereotypes Can Be Unconscious but Reversible, Stanford GSB (http://gsb.stanford.edu/news/research/hr_racialstereotypes.shtml)
  - Stereotyping from the Perspective of Perceivers and Targets, Online Readings in Psychology and Culture (Unit 15, Chapter 3), Western Washington University (http://www.ac.wwu.edu/~culture/Khan.htm

EXPANSION ACTIVITY: Infinitives of Purpose

- Have students go online and find the results of a study about stereotypes. Brainstorm or present a list of helpful search terms *(stereotype studies, the effects of stereotypes, research on stereotypes)*. Remind students that .edu (education) and .gov (government) sites are usually more reliable than some .com (commercial) sites.
- Have students write a summary of the research they found, using at least one infinitive of purpose.
- Ask students to give an oral summary of the research they found.

PART 4 THE MECHANICS OF WRITING, PAGES 130–134

- Go over the directions.

Using the Word *When*

- Go over the information in the box about using the word *when*. Ask: *When do we need to use a comma with* when?

A. Practice: Using the Word *When*

- Go over the directions.
- Have students write sentences to answer the questions using the word *when.*
- Put students in pairs to compare sentences.
- Call on volunteers to read their sentences to the class.

ANSWER KEY

Answers will vary.

Using the Word *So*

- Go over the information in the box.

B. Practice: Using the Word *So*

- Go over the directions and the example.
- Have students combine the sentences using *so.*
- Have students check their answers with a partner.
- Go over the answers with the class.

ANSWER KEY

1. I was a girl, so my parents gave me typical girls' toys.
2. I had two brothers, so there were a lot of toys for boys around the house.
3. We lived far from other houses, so there weren't many other girls to play with.
4. There weren't a lot of children around, so I played with my brothers.
5. I played with my brothers, so I learned typical boys' games from them.

Review: Conjunctions

- Go over the information in the box.
- Ask comprehension questions, such as: *What conjunction do we use to join opposite things or ideas? What conjunction do we use for similar ideas? When do we use the conjunction* or*? When do we use a comma?*

C. Practice: Conjunctions

- Go over the directions and the example.
- Have students combine the sentences.
- Have students check their answers with a partner.
- Go over the answers with the class.

ANSWER KEY

1. We ran, jumped, and swam.
2. I played with my sister, and I played with the kids in the neighborhood. *AND* I played with my sister and the kids in the neighborhood.
3. We didn't watch much TV or go to the movies.
4. We had fun, but we didn't have a lot of toys. *AND* We had fun but not a lot of toys.
5. We played outside, or we played inside on rainy days. *AND* We played outside, but we played inside on rainy days.
6. I played with both boys and girls, so I practiced both social language and the language of tasks.
7. I was the writer, director, and star of the movie.
8. I was happy, but the other kids weren't.

EXPANSION ACTIVITY: Match Up

❍ Photocopy the Black Line Master *Match Up* on page BLM 7. Make enough copies for each pair of students.
❍ Cut each sheet along the dotted lines and put the strips in an envelope.
❍ Have students form pairs. Give a set of strips to each pair of students.
❍ Have students work in pairs to match the strips.
❍ Call on students to read the completed sentences to the class.

ANSWER KEY

1. Girls often play games that involve conversation, but boys often use problem-solving in games.
2. Chimps need to get termites to eat, so they use twigs as tools.
3. Female chimps spend more time with their mothers, so they learn how to use the twigs faster.
4. Male chimps hunt to get meat, but they don't always share.
5. Gender differences can be affected by our genes, or they can be learned.
6. Toys can influence how much children talk, and how active the children are.
7. Parents can't change their children's genes, but they can affect what toys children use.
8. Some parents want to help daughters prepare for a career, so they give them boys' toys.
9. Parents may want their boys to prepare for a career, but they also want them to prepare for relationships.
10. Some stereotypes are negative, and they negatively affect how well the targets do on certain tasks.
11. Positive stereotypes can be helpful, but negative ones usually cause harm.
12. There are stereotypes about age, and there are stereotypes about gender.

Using the Phrase *Used To*

❍ Go over the information in the box.

D. Practice: Using the Phrase *Used To*

❍ Go over the directions.
❍ Have students stand and move around the classroom, asking classmates the questions in the chart. Remind students to record the answers on the chart.
❍ Call on students to tell the class about a classmate's answers.

ANSWER KEY

Answers will vary.

Finding Words in Phrases

❍ Go over the information in the box. Ask: *What are some types of phrases?*

E. Practice: Finding Words in Phrases

❍ Go over the directions. Remind students to look for the types of phrases in the box.
❍ Read the first sentence. Elicit the phrase that should be underlined (*reminded the students of*). Ask what type of phrase it is (*verb + noun + preposition*).
❍ Have students underline the phrases and then check their answers with a partner.
❍ Go over the answers with the class.

ANSWER KEY

1. reminded the students of; 2. purpose of the study; 3. cause of the problem; 4. test of memory; 5. fill out a questionnaire; 6. stereotype of Xenrovians; 7. protected them from danger; 8. results of the study; 9. think of this game/practice for adulthood; 10. came to the conclusion/have an effect on us

TOEFL® iBT Tip

TOEFL iBT TIP 5: Although the TOEFL iBT does not discretely test grammar skills, examinees' essay scores will be determined based on the range of grammar and vocabulary used in their essays.

❍ Point out that the grammar activities in *The Mechanics of Writing* part of this chapter will help them improve the organization and coherence of their essays.

❍ TOEFL iBT essays may be scored higher based on whether or not the examinee can use subordination in a sentence. Using conjunctions and connectors and more sophisticated phrases will help students improve their overall essay writing.

F. Review: Editing a Paragraph

❍ Go over the directions.
❍ Have students find and correct the six mistakes. Have them check their answers with a partner.
❍ Go over the answers with the class.

ANSWER KEY

When Jane Goodall was 26 years old ^, Louis Leakey sent her to Tanzania. The purpose of her study was to learn about the wild chimps. She wasn't afraid ~~about~~ ^of them ^, but they were afraid of her. She use^d to take her binoculars/ and sit for many hours every day. Finally, after many months, they let her get close. For almost forty years, she studied the chimps of Gombe. Today, from Goodall's research, we know about chimps' ability to use tools, to be effective mothers ^, and to learn new things.

PART 5 ACADEMIC WRITING, PAGES 135–139

Writing Assignment

❍ Go over the directions.

Model

❍ Have students read the six steps of the example.
❍ Direct students' attention to Step A of the example, and ask: *What topic did the student choose?*
❍ Direct students' attention to Step B. Ask: *What questions did the student use to get ideas? What specific details does the writer mention? How did the writer put the steps in order?*
❍ Direct students' attention to Step C. Elicit examples of conjunctions used to combine ideas.
❍ Have students read the paragraph in Step D of the example. Ask: *How did the writer combine sentences in the paragraph?*
❍ Direct students' attention to Step E. Ask: *How many mistakes did the writer circle in the paragraph in Step D? What are they?*
❍ Have students read the paragraph in Step F. Ask: *How did the writer correct the mistakes?*

Your Turn

❍ Have students read Step A and choose a topic.
❍ Have students answer the questions in Step B. You may want to put students in pairs to discuss their ideas.
❍ Have students complete Steps C and D. If you want to have your students practice peer editing skills, have them exchange paragraphs with a partner and comment on mistakes or other problems.

WRITING STRATEGY: Editing Your Paragraph

❍ Go over the information in the box. Ask: *What are two types of mistakes?*

TOEFL® iBT Tip

TOEFL iBT TIP 6: Both the integrated and independent essays of the TOEFL iBT will be scored based on how well the examinee completes the overall writing task. However, the writing section also requires that the essay follow the conventions of spelling, punctuation, and layout.

- Point out that the *Editing Your Paragraph* strategy in the *Academic Writing* part of this chapter will help students improve their coherence and ability to link the flow of ideas in their essays.

(**Your Turn**, *continued*)

- Ask students to edit their paragraphs (Step E) and then rewrite (Step F).
- Collect the paragraphs.

EXPANSION ACTIVITY: Editing Practice

- Photocopy the Black Line Master *Editing Practice* on page BLM 8 and distribute to students.
- Have students make the corrections and then compare paragraphs with a partner.
- Go over the corrections with the class.

ANSWER KEY

When I was young, my parents used to play~~ing~~ cards a lot. I didn't like cards, ~~and~~ but I liked to read. When my parents tried to get me to play cards with them, I used to refuse. I didn't want to waste my time. Now I have children. I enjoy playing games with them. Surprisingly, I even enjoy playing cards. I don't really like the card games, but I like the conversations we have/ when we play. There is sometimes more to a game than I thought. When parents and children play a game together, they can have a stronger relationship.

UNIT 3 SOCIOLOGY

CHAPTER 6 BECOMING A MEMBER OF A COMMUNITY

In this chapter, students will read about when and how people are judged to be an adult in different cultures. In the first reading, students will learn the ages at which people in different countries are able to participate in adult activities such as voting, driving, and getting married. Students will then read about rites of passage, how young people become members of a group, and the characteristics of these coming-of-age rituals. Finally, students will explore three specific coming-of-age traditions: Coming-of-Age Day in Japan, *fiesta de quinceaños* in Latino cultures, and *rumspringa* in the Amish society in the United States. The Amish are a religious group in the United States who follow strict rules about clothing and appropriate behavior and avoid most aspects of modern society. These topics will prepare students to write about a rite of passage or ritual that they know.

VOCABULARY

appropriate	elegant	individuals	population	strict
at this point	escort	initiation	rejoin	symbolizes
club	explore	incorporation	rituals	tiara
condition	farms	lifestyle	separation	transition
dating	fewer	military	social position	tuxedo
either	horse-drawn buggies	participate in	stages	

READING STRATEGIES

Guessing the Meanings of New Words: *Or*
Recognizing Key Words
Using Topic Sentences to Preview
Guessing the Meanings of New Words: Pictures and Captions
Finding Details
Understanding Words in Phrases: Verbs + Prepositions

CRITICAL THINKING STRATEGIES

Supporting Opinions with Experiences (Part 1)
Classifying (Part 2)
Making Comparisons (Part 3)
Synthesizing (Part 3)
Note: The strategy in bold is highlighted in the student book.

MECHANICS

Review: The Simple Present Tense
Review: Subject-Verb Agreement
Requirements: *Must* and *Have To*
Review: Showing Order
Prepositions of Place
Words in Phrases: Verb + Preposition Combinations

WRITING STRATEGY

Rewriting Your Paragraph

CHAPTER 6 Becoming a Member of a Community

Chapter 6 Opener, page 141

- ❍ Direct students' attention to the photo. Ask them what is happening in the photo.
- ❍ Have students discuss the four questions. This can be done in pairs, in small groups, or as a class.
- ❍ Check students' predictions of the chapter topic.

PART 1 INTRODUCTION BECOMING AN ADULT, PAGES 142–144

Before Reading

Thinking Ahead

- ❍ Have students look at the photos. Check comprehension by asking questions: *What is the man doing in the first photo? At what age can you vote in Thailand? What age do you have to be to drive in the second photo?*
- ❍ Put students in pairs to answer the questions.
- ❍ Call on students to share their answers with the class.

ANSWER KEY

Answers will vary.

Reading

- ❍ Go over the directions and the question.
- ❍ Have students read the passage silently, or have students follow along silently as you play the audio program.
- ❍ Ask students what events are a sign of adulthood.

After Reading

A. Check Your Understanding

- ❍ Go over the directions.
- ❍ Have students fill in the correct bubble and then check their answers with a partner.
- ❍ Go over the answers with the class. For additional practice, have students correct the false statements.

ANSWER KEY

1. T; 2. F; 3. F; 4. T; 5. F

Corrections of False Statements:

2. Young people can vote once they turn 17 in Korea.
3. A 17-year-old girl can get married with parental consent in Thailand.
5. Bulgarians can drive at age 18.

Culture Note:

- ❍ You may want to point out that in the United States, the ages at which you are legally allowed to do some things are determined by the state, rather than the federal government. Driving ages and marriage ages are different in different states.

B. Talk About It

- ❍ Go over the directions.
- ❍ Put students in small groups to answer the questions.
- ❍ Call on students to share their ideas with the class.

ANSWER KEY

Answers will vary.

CRITICAL THINKING STRATEGY: Supporting Opinions with Experiences

- ❍ You may want to point out that an important critical thinking strategy is the ability to support opinions. Explain or elicit that such support can come from facts, experts, or our own experience.
- ❍ In Activity B, students talked about their opinions. In the following Expansion Activity, *Agree or Disagree?*, they can practice supporting opinions.

EXPANSION ACTIVITY: Agree or Disagree?

- Write *Agree* on one side of the board or room and *Disagree* on the other.
- Have a group of students come to the front of the room.
- Explain the activity: you will say a statement, and students should move to stand near the word that best expresses their position.
- Say: *People should be able to vote at the same age as they are able to get married.* Remind students to move to express their opinions.
- When students have moved, call on students to explain their positions. Remind them to use support from their own experiences *(I agree. My parents got married at 16, and they were both mature. I think if they are old enough to support themselves and a family, they're old enough to vote.)*.
- Say two more statements, and then call another group of students to the board.
- Continue until all students have had a chance to support their opinions.
- Create your own statements or use the ones below.
  Teenagers are too young to get married.
  Young people should be required to stay in school until they finish secondary school.
  Getting married requires the same maturity as driving.
  If people can serve in the army, they should be able to vote.
  Voting requires better judgment than getting married.
  Young people in some countries are generally more mature than young people of the same age in other countries.

PART 2 GENERAL INTEREST READING
RITES OF PASSAGE, PAGES 144–149

Before Reading

A. Thinking Ahead

- Go over the directions.
- Have students choose an event and answer the questions.
- Have students stand and move around the classroom, asking four classmates the questions for the event that they have chosen. Point out that they are going to be asking different people about different events. Students should write classmates' answers on the chart.
- Call on students to tell the class about an event a classmate chose and what they found out from their classmates.

ANSWER KEY

Answers will vary.

EXPANSION ACTIVITY: Presentations

- Put students in pairs or small groups.
- Have each group choose a country and an event to research as an out-of-class activity (e.g., *weddings in Italy*). Tell students they can ask questions of people from that country, as well as do research online or at the library.
- Tell groups they will give a five-minute presentation to the class on their topic. They should use the questions in Activity A as a starting point. You may need to give students a couple of days to complete their research and prepare the presentation.
- After students have prepared, have each group present the information to the class.

B. Vocabulary Preparation

- Go over the directions. Have students look at the definitions. Explain unfamiliar terms if necessary.
- If students need more help with pronunciation, read the sentences aloud and have students repeat.
- Go over the example. Have students match the definitions to the words in color by writing the letters on the lines next to the sentences.
- Have students check their answers with a partner.
- Go over the answers with the class.

ANSWER KEY

1. g; 2. e; 3. c 4. f; 5. d; 6. b; 7. a

EXPANSION ACTIVITY: Sentence Challenge

- Have students write sentences using all the words in Activity B. Point out that the sentences must use the words correctly, but that the emphasis is on using all the words in as few sentences as possible.
- Put students in pairs to read their sentences to each other. Remind students to help their partners edit and correct mistakes.
- Call on students to read their sentences to the class.

READING STRATEGY: Guessing the Meanings of New Words: *Or*

- Go over the information in the box.

C. Guessing the Meanings of New Words: *Or*

- Go over the directions.
- Have students look over the first paragraph. Elicit examples of definitions that are before or after the word *or (rites of passage, rituals)*.

Reading

- Go over the directions and the question.
- Have students read the passage silently, or have students follow along silently as you play the audio program.
- Ask students: *What are some rites of passage?*

EXPANSION ACTIVITY: Listen For It

- Point out that sometimes important words or phrases are repeated throughout a reading.
- Divide the class in half. Assign one half the target phrase *rite of passage,* and the other half the target word *ritual.* Note that students might hear the plural form of their target word or phrase *(rites of passage, rituals)*.
- Explain the activity: You will play the audio program. Whenever students hear their target word or phrase, they must stand if they are sitting and sit if they are standing.
- Play the audio program. The first time you hear a target word or phrase, pause and remind students who were assigned that word or phrase to stand. The first target word or phrase students will hear is *rite of passage.* Make sure those students assigned this target phrase stand.
- Remind students the next time they hear their target phrase they should sit. Tell the other half of the students to do the same with their target word. Continue playing the audio program. Note that each group will stand and sit more than once.
- This activity is meant to highlight keywords (the reading strategy on page 149 in the student book) and get students moving.

After Reading

A. Check Your Understanding

- Go over the directions.
- Have students check the statements that are true.
- Go over the answers with the class.

ANSWER KEY

Check: 1, 3, 5

CRITICAL THINKING STRATEGY: Classifying

❍ Point out that classifying, or putting things in groups, is an important critical thinking strategy. It allows us to notice what things have in common and to make connections between ideas.

B. Finding Details

❍ Go over the directions.
❍ Have students complete the tree diagram and then compare their ideas with a partner.
❍ Call on students to share their ideas with the class.

ANSWER KEY

Characteristic 1: special clothing
Example 1: bride's wedding dress
Example 2: graduation cap and tassel
Example 3: baby's naming ritual dress
Characteristic 2: groups
Example 1: military
Example 2: graduates
Characteristic 3: difficult or challenging experience
Example 1: apache girl dances for many hours and doesn't eat for four days
Example 2: in some religions, young people must memorize something

TOEFL® iBT Tip

TOEFL iBT TIP 1: The TOEFL iBT tests the ability to understand key facts and the important information contained within a text. Locating key words in a text will help students build vocabulary and improve their reading skills.

❍ Point out that the *Critical Thinking Strategy* on classifying or making connections between ideas can help students prepare for the classification or summary question type.

❍ In addition, the *Finding Details* activity requires students to connect and organize information in using a graphic organizer. This will help to scaffold students' abilities upward toward mastering the schematic table questions on the test.

C. Vocabulary Check

❍ Direct students' attention to the words in the box. Say each word and have students repeat.
❍ Go over the directions and the example.
❍ Have students fill in the blanks and then check their answers with a partner.
❍ Go over the answers with the class.

ANSWER KEY

1. transition; 2. rituals; 3. club; 4. symbolizes; 5. appropriate; 6. stages

EXPANSION ACTIVITY: Your Experience

❍ Have students choose three vocabulary words from Activity C and write a sentence for each word that tells something about their own personal experience.
❍ Put students in pairs to read their sentences to each other.
❍ Call on students to tell the class something about their partner *(Lee joined an archaeology club last year.)*.

READING STRATEGY: Recognizing Key Words

❍ Go over the information in the box. Ask: *What are key words? How can we recognize them?*

D. Practice: Recognizing Key Words

❍ Go over the directions.
❍ Have students answer the questions and then check their answers with a partner.
❍ Go over the answers.

ANSWER KEY

1. separation, transition, incorporation; 2. separation; 3. transition; 4. they acquire their new role and rejoin the group

E. Talk About It

❍ Go over the directions.
❍ Put students in pairs to describe a rite of passage that they know about, using the questions as a guide.
❍ Call on students to tell the class about the rite of passage.

ANSWER KEY

Answers will vary.

EXPANSION ACTIVITY: Graphic Organizer

❍ Have students create a graphic organizer for the rite of passage they described in Activity E. Remind students to use the graphic organizer in Activity B as a model—with characteristics and examples.

PART  ACADEMIC READING COMING-OF-AGE RITUALS, PAGES 150–156

Before Reading

READING STRATEGY: Using Topic Sentences to Preview

❍ Go over the information in the box.
❍ Ask: *What is one way you can preview a reading? Why is the first sentence of a paragraph often important?*

A. Using Topic Sentences to Preview

❍ Go over the directions.
❍ Have students read the topic sentences and answer the questions with a partner.
❍ Call on students to share their answers with the class.

ANSWER KEY

1. Japan, Latino cultures, the Amish; 2. the reason for the event, the dress, and the activities; 3. the transition to adulthood in three different cultures

TOEFL® iBT Tip

TOEFL iBT TIP 2: The TOEFL iBT does not directly test the ability to determine the main idea in a text. Instead, examinees are required to recognize the minor, less important ideas that do not belong in a summary; or, they may be required to distinguish between major and minor points of information.

❍ Point out that the strategy for *Using Topic Sentences to Preview* will help students distinguish between major and minor points in a text on the TOEFL iBT and link those ideas throughout the passage.

❍ Remind students that this type of question is called a *prose summary* or *classification* question, and partial credit will be given for correct answers. On the TOEFL iBT, the answers to this type of question are not in traditional multiple-choice format.

The question type appears in the form of a schematic table that requires examinees to select and drag answer choices to specific positions in a chart.

B. Vocabulary Preparation

❍ Go over the directions and the example.
❍ Have students match the definitions to the words and then check their answers with a partner.
❍ Go over the answers with the class.

ANSWER KEY

1. c; 2. d; 3. a; 4. f; 5. g; 6. b; 7. e

READING STRATEGY: Guessing the Meanings of New Words: Pictures and Captions

- Go over the information in the box.
- Have students write a definition for the word *tassel,* using the information in the picture and caption.
- Call on students to read their definitions to the class.

C. Guessing the Meanings of New Words: Pictures and Captions

- Go over the directions.
- Have students look at the photos and captions and identify vocabulary words *(tassel, elegant, tiara, tuxedo, escort, horse-drawn buggy).*

TOEFL® iBT Tip

TOEFL iBT TIP 3: The TOEFL iBT measures the ability to understand specific words and phrases selected by the author and used in the passage.

- Point out that the strategy and activity for *Guessing the Meanings of New Words: Pictures and Captions* will help students improve their vocabulary for the TOEFL iBT. Often, a passage may be accompanied by an image, drawing, or table to help the examinee better understand the passage.

Reading

- Go over the directions and the question.
- Have students read the passage silently, or play the audio program and have students follow along silently.

EXPANSION ACTIVITY: Thought Groups

- Explain that students can improve their comprehension and be more easily understood when speaking if they notice and practice using thought groups. Thought groups are the phrases that native speakers say at one time as a group, in one breath. For example, in the sentence, *The girl dances first with her father and then with each of the male guests,* many native speakers would pause between *father* and *and.* These pauses are often marked with punctuation, but not always.
- Tell students you are going to play the audio program again and as they follow along, students should put a slash between words whenever they hear a pause.
- Play the audio program. After each paragraph, elicit where students noticed pauses that were not marked by punctuation.
- Point out the types of structures that often form thought groups (*prepositional phrases, noun phrases, clauses, verb and object combinations).*

After Reading

A. Check Your Understanding

- Go over the directions.
- Have students check the true statements and then check their answers with a partner.
- Go over the answers with the class.
- For additional practice, have students correct the false statements.

ANSWER KEY

Check: 1

Corrected False Statements:

2. Coming-of-Age is celebrated by fewer people every year, and the government celebrations are less popular.
3. The *quinceaños* is a very formal event.
4. The tiara symbolizes the girl's adulthood.
5. Most Amish teens return to their families after *rumspringa.*

READING STRATEGY: Finding Details

- Go over the information in the box.
- Ask: *What are some details that follow main idea statements?*

B. Practice: Finding Details

- Go over the directions.
- Have students complete the chart.
- Put students in pairs to compare answers.
- Go over the answers with the class.

ANSWER KEY

Ideas	Details
In Japan, 20-year-olds have the rights of adults.	They can vote, and get married without parental consent.
For Coming-of-Age Day, young adults wear formal clothing.	Some women wear beautiful kimonos and white fur collars. Young men usually wear business suits.
Fiesta de quinceaños is a very formal event.	It's similar to a big church wedding. Everyone wears formal clothing—tuxedos and elegant party dresses. The *quinceañera* wears a long white or pink dress.
For the *quinceaños* celebration, the girl receives symbolic gifts.	One is a tiara, a small crown. The tiara means the girl is special, like a princess. A family member puts the tiara on the girl's head. This symbolizes her adulthood.
The Amish have strict rules.	Amish wear dark clothes. Many women wear long dresses. Most Amish do not own cars. Instead they ride in horse-drawn buggies. Most do not allow electricity in their homes. Most do not allow their photograph to be taken.
Most Amish teen-agers return to the Amish way of life.	85–90% return to their families, their values, and the Amish lifestyle.

TOEFL® iBT Tip

TOEFL iBT TIP 4: The TOEFL iBT tests the ability to understand facts, examples, and explanations in a text; however, it does not directly test understanding of the main idea of a passage.

- The *Finding Details* activity requires students to connect information in a graphic organizer. This will help to scaffold students' abilities upward toward mastering the schematic table questions on the test.
- Remind students that being able to skim and scan to locate information is a technique that will help them with the schematic table question type on the test.

C. Vocabulary Check

- Go over the directions and the example.
- Have students complete the sentences and then check their answers with a partner.
- Go over the answers with the class.

ANSWER KEY

1. tuxedo; 2. dating; 3. escort; 4. tiara; 5. horse-drawn buggies; 6. farms

EXPANSION ACTIVITY: Crossword Puzzle

- Photocopy the Black Line Master *Crossword Puzzle* on page BLM 9 and distribute it to students.
- Have students complete the crossword and then compare answers with a partner.
- Go over the answers with the class.

ANSWER KEY

Across:
1. participate; 3. military; 4. either; 5. elegant; 6. condition; 7. lifestyle
Down:
1. population; 2. individual; 5. explore

READING STRATEGY: Understanding Words in Phrases: Verbs + Prepositions

- Go over the information in the box.
- Elicit examples of verb + preposition combinations. Point out that sometimes these combinations have a meaning that is quite different from the words taken by themselves.

 D. Practice: Words in Phrases

- Go over the directions.
- Have students find and underline the verb + preposition combinations in *Coming-of-Age Rituals.*
- Have students match the phrasal verbs with their meanings.
- Go over the answers with the class.

ANSWER KEY

1. c; 2. b; 3. d; 4. a

CRITICAL THINKING STRATEGY: Making Comparisons

- Go over the information in the box.

E. Practice: Making Comparisons

- Go over the directions.
- Put students in small groups. Have students complete the chart and discuss with their group.
- Go over the answers with the class.

ANSWER KEY

	Coming-of-Age Day	Fiesta de *Quinceaños*	*Rumspringa*
Purpose or Reason	adulthood	adulthood	adulthood
For boys, girls, or both	both	girls	both
Age for ritual	20	15	16
Special clothes	yes (kimonos and business suits)	yes (elegant clothes)	no, but they don't have to wear Amish clothes
Symbolic gifts	no (they receive gifts, but they aren't symbolic)	yes (tiara)	no
Party	yes	yes	maybe
Photo-graphs	yes	yes	no

EXPANSION ACTIVITY: Practice Conjunctions

- Remind students that they can talk about similarities using the conjunction *and* (*The* fiesta de quinceaños *celebrates adulthood, and* rumspringa *celebrates adulthood, too. OR The* fiesta de quinceaños *and* rumspringa *celebrate adulthood.*). They can talk about differences using the conjunction *but* (Rumspringa *is for both boys and girls, but the* fiesta de quinceaños *is only for girls.*).
- Call on a student and say a category *(age)* and two events (*Coming-of-Age Day* and *rumspringa*). Elicit a comparison sentence using the conjunction *and* or *but.*
- Continue with other students, or put the students in pairs to take turns prompting and saying sentences.

CRITICAL THINKING STRATEGY: Synthesizing

- Remind students that when they put together information from different sources, they are synthesizing (as in Activity F).

TOEFL® iBT Tip

TOEFL iBT TIP 5: The TOEFL iBT tests the ability to read a passage, listen to a lecture related to that passage, and then write in response to a question based on the two stimuli. This integrated writing skill requires students to think critically about material that they have read, interpret that information and relate it to a lecture, then present ideas in essay format.

- Remind students that making comparisons between things and synthesizing the information can be further applied in the next parts of this chapter: *The Mechanics of Writing* and *Academic Writing.*

F. Making Connections

- Go over the directions.
- Put students in pairs. Have students choose a ritual from the reading *Coming-of-Age Rituals* and answer the questions.
- Call on students to share their ideas with the class.

ANSWER KEY

Answers will vary.

EXPANSION ACTIVITY: Chart It

- Have students create a chart with headings like the one in Activity E. In the first column, have students write the questions from Activity F.
- Have students complete the chart with information from the reading and then compare charts with a partner. Point out that they are simply making notes on the same information from the reading in chart form.

G. Journal Writing

- Go over the directions. Have students choose a topic.
- Explain that this is a quick-writing activity and does not have to be perfect. Point out that journal writing can be a warm-up to a more structured writing assignment, helping to generate ideas.
- Have students write. Set a time limit of five minutes.
- Put students in pairs to read or talk about their writing.

Website Research

- For additional information on rites of passage and coming-of-age rituals, you could direct students to the following websites:
  - Coming of Age Rituals, Gallaudet University (http://edf3.gallaudet.edu/diversity/BGG/RitesofPassage)
  - Making the Grade—African Arts of Initiation, Coming of Age (http://www.nmafa.si.edu/exhibits/nkanu/botmak.htm)
  - Borderlands: A hispanic girl's coming of age (http://www.epcc.edu/ftp/Homes/monicaw/borderlands/10_a_hispanic_girl's.htm)
  - Rites of Passage—Traditional Religions, Story of Africa (BBC) (http://www.bbc.co.uk/worldservice/africa/features/storyofafrica/6chapter3.shtml)
  - Rites of Passage Tutorials—Dennis O'neil, Palomar College (http://anthro.palomar.edu/social/soc_4.htm)

PART 4 THE MECHANICS OF WRITING, PAGES 157–160

- Go over the directions.

Review: The Simple Present Tense/Review: Subject-Verb Agreement

- Review the information in the box about the simple present and subject-verb agreement. Ask: *When do we use the simple present?*

A. Practice: The Simple Present Tense

- Go over the directions.
- Have students complete the sentences with the correct forms of the verbs in parentheses.
- Put students in pairs to check their answers.
- Call on volunteers to write the words on the board or say them out loud to the class.

ANSWER KEY

1. means; 2. has; 3. attend; 4. celebrate; 5. wear; 6. dance; 7. are; is

Requirements: *Must* and *Have To*

- Go over the information in the box. Make sure students understand the meanings of *necessary* and *required.*
- Ask questions such as: *Do we have to eat breakfast every day? What is something you must do before you can drive legally?*

B. Practice: Requirements: *Must* and *Have To*

- Go over the directions.
- Have students choose a rite of passage that they know and write six sentences about what is required in this rite of passage.
- Call on students to tell the class about the rite of passage they know.

ANSWER KEY

Answers will vary.

EXPANSION ACTIVITY: Group Presentations

- Put students in pairs or small groups. Have students choose a culture and a rite of passage to research.
- Direct students to the websites listed on page 79 of the Teacher's Edition, or have students use a search engine and enter the phrases "rites of passage" or "coming of age rituals." Remind students that sites ending in .edu (educational sites) and .gov (government sites) are sometimes more reliable than sites that end with .com (commercial sites).
- Tell students to prepare a three to five minute presentation on the chosen topic, using information they learned from their website research. Remind students to use *must* and *have to* in their presentations.
- Have students present to the class.

Review: Showing Order

- Go over the information in the box. Ask: *What are some order words? What order word should not have a comma?*

C. Review: Showing Order

- Go over the directions.
- Have students write a paragraph using the sentences and order words.
- Put students in pairs to take turns reading their paragraphs aloud.
- Call on students to read their paragraphs to the class.

ANSWER KEY

Answers will vary, although the order of the events should match the sequence in the book. Make sure students use order words.

Prepositions of Place

- Go over the information in the box.
- Ask comprehension questions, such as: *What prepositions do we use with body parts and places? Do we put a hat on or in our heads? Do we walk on the classroom or around the classroom?*

D. Practice: Prepositions of Place

- Go over the directions.
- Direct students' attention to the illustration on page 159. Ask questions: *What are they wearing on their heads? What is the girl doing on the far right side?*
- Have students write sentences using prepositions of place.
- Have students compare sentences with a partner.
- Call on students to read their sentences to the class.

ANSWER KEY

Answers will vary. Examples of possible answers include:
They are wearing caps on their heads.
There are tassels on the caps.
They are dressed in gowns.
She is holding something in her hand.
They are walking across the stage.
They are standing in a room.
They are walking across the room.

Words in Phrases: Verb + Preposition Combinations

- Go over the information in the box.

Vocabulary Note:

- You may want to point out that it is easier to remember and use new vocabulary when we learn it as part of a phrase. Learning vocabulary as part of a phrase can help non-native speakers become more fluent.

E. Practice: Words in Phrases

- Go over the directions and the example.
- Have students underline the phrases in the rest of the sentences.
- Have students check their answers with a partner.
- Go over the answers with the class.

ANSWER KEY

1. put on; 2. takes off; 3. turns off; 4. turn on; 5. stand up; 6. sit down; 7. move out

EXPANSION ACTIVITY: Charades

- Have students brainstorm a list of verb + preposition combinations and write the list on the board. Include all the words from Activity E and any others the students know.
- Call a volunteer to the front of the room. Whisper a verb + preposition combination (e.g., *put on*) to the volunteer.
- Have the volunteer silently act out the verb + preposition combination. Elicit the phrase from the class.
- Continue with other volunteers and phrases.

F. Review: Editing a Paragraph

- Go over the directions.
- Have students find and correct the mistakes. Have them check their answers with a partner.
- Go over the answers with the class.

ANSWER KEY

A traditional coming-of-age ceremony for an Apache girl is the Sunrise Dance. For this ritual, an Apache girl ~~have~~ has many challenging tasks. First, she must ~~awake~~ wake up very early in the morning. She puts on a special dress. Then/she ~~must~~ dances and sings for several hours. Then she must run in four directions. After that, a medicine man blesses her. At the end, the girl throws a blanket in four directions. At this point, the ceremony is over.

Note: *The sentence "Then she must dances and sings for several hours" can also be corrected as "Then she must dance and sing for several hours."*

PART 5 ACADEMIC WRITING, PAGES 161–165

Writing Assignment

❍ Go over the directions.

Model

❍ Have students read the six steps of the example.
❍ Direct students' attention to Step A of the example, and ask: *What topic did the student choose?*
❍ Direct students' attention to Step B. Ask: *What kind of ritual is it? What does the writer include to describe what happens? What are the characteristics that the writer looks at?*
❍ Direct students' attention to Step C. Ask questions: *What do they wear? Where do they sit? What do students do when they hear their name?*
❍ Have students read the paragraph in Step D of the example. Ask questions: *What is the topic sentence? What details does the writer include? What words does the writer use to show order?*
❍ Direct students' attention to Step E. Ask: *How many mistakes did the writer circle in the paragraph in Step D? What are they?*
❍ Have students read the paragraph in Step F. Ask: *How did the writer correct the mistakes?*

Your Turn

❍ Have students read Step A and choose a topic.
❍ Have students answer the questions in Step B. You may want to put students in pairs to discuss their ideas.
❍ Have students complete Steps C and D. If you want to have your students practice peer editing skills, have them exchange paragraphs with a partner and comment on mistakes or other problems.
❍ Ask students to edit their paragraphs (Step E).

WRITING STRATEGY: Rewriting Your Paragraph

❍ Go over the information in the box. Ask: *What questions can you ask yourself when you rewrite?*

TOEFL® iBT Tip

TOEFL iBT TIP 6: The integrated writing skill on the TOEFL iBT requires students to think critically about material that they have read, interpret that information and relate it to a lecture, then present ideas in essay format.

❍ Remind students that the *Rewriting Your Paragraph* strategy corresponds to a strategy they will need to use when writing their essays. They will be able to take notes and summarize ideas in a reading passage, or create a brief outline before they write an independent essay.

❍ Students should leave themselves time to read over their work and edit for mistakes, particularly if they choose to type the essay on the computer.

(**Your Turn**, *continued*)
❍ Have students rewrite their paragraphs (Step F).
❍ Collect the paragraphs.

EXPANSION ACTIVITY: Jigsaw

❍ Put students in small groups according to the type of ritual they selected for their writing *(naming, initiation, coming-of-age, graduation, or wedding)*.
❍ Have students in each group read their paragraphs and give comments on paragraphs of other students in the group.
❍ Ask students to note similarities and differences among the rituals within the group.
❍ Put students in new groups, this time grouping students with different types of rituals. Try to have one representative of each type of ritual in each group.
❍ Have students share the information they learned of similarities and differences in their first small group with their new group members.
❍ Walk around to monitor the activity and provide help as needed. Ask questions: *How are naming rituals similar? What do initiation rituals have in common? How are coming-of-age ceremonies different from graduations?*

Unit 3 Vocabulary Workshop

- Have students review vocabulary from Chapters 5–6.

A. Matching

- Go over the directions.
- Have students write the correct letters on the lines to match the definitions with the words.
- Go over the answers.

ANSWER KEY

1. e; 2. g; 3. f; 4. h; 5. c; 6. i; 7. j; 8. a; 9. b; 10. d

B. True or False?

- Go over the directions.
- Have students fill in the correct bubbles.
- Go over the answers.

ANSWER KEY

1. F; 2. T; 3. T; 4. F; 5. T; 6. F; 7. F; 8. T

C. Sentence Halves

- Go over the directions.
- Have students match the first halves of the sentences with the correct second halves.
- Go over the answers.

ANSWER KEY

1. f; 2. e; 3. a; 4. b; 5. d; 6. c

D. Words in Phrases: Prepositions

- Go over the directions.
- Have students fill in the blanks with the correct prepositions. Note that students will use two of the prepositions more than once.
- Go over the answers.

ANSWER KEY

1. out; 2. to; 3. on; 4. in; 5. on; 6. to; 7. up; 8. of

Name: ______________________ **Date:** ______________

Find Someone Who

Directions: Take this paper and a pencil. Stand up and move around the classroom. Ask classmates about the questions below. When someone answers *yes*, write his or her name on the line. When someone answers *no*, ask another question. If no one answers *yes*, write "no one" on the line.

Example: A: *Do you have two or more sisters?*
B: *Yes, I do.*
A: *Great. What's your name?*

Questions:	**Name:**
Do you have two or more sisters?	______________
Do you have a younger brother or a younger sister?	______________
Do you have older brothers?	______________
Do you live with your parents?	______________
Are there twins in your family?	______________
Are you a twin?	______________
Are you the youngest in the family?	______________
Are you the oldest in the family?	______________
Are you very independent?	______________
Are you shy?	______________
Are you very friendly?	______________

Name: ______________________________ **Date:** ______________

Family Characteristics

Directions: Compare yourself with someone in your family. Write characteristics only you have in the circle on the left, characteristics you share with the family member in the middle circle, and characteristics that only your family member has in the circle on the right.

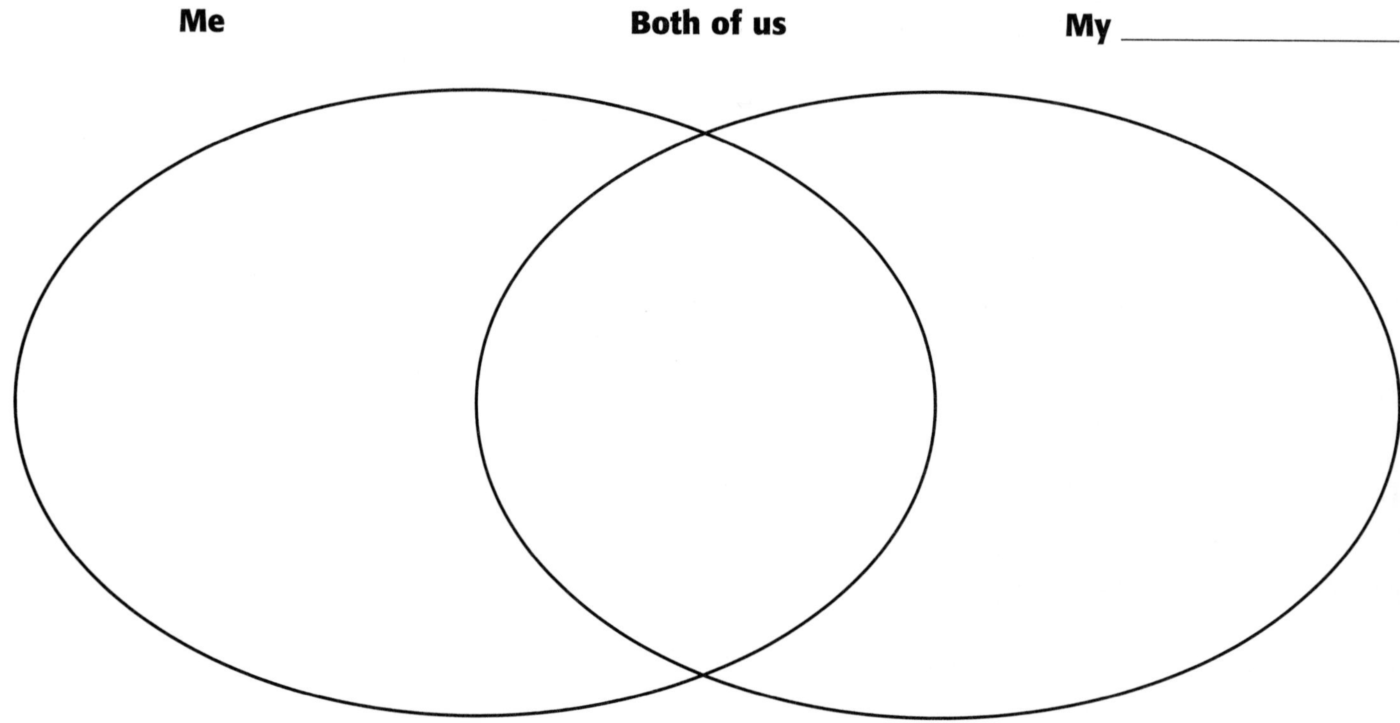

Reconstruction

Part 1: Introduction

Teaching methods change over time.

Eric Jensen wrote *Teaching with the Brain in Mind* about the brain and learning.

Part 2: Learning and the Brain

Genes determine 30–60 percent of brain connections.

Education and life experience determine 40–70 percent of brain connections.

The brain cells of both children and adults grow new connections in a rich environment.

Part 3: What is a "Rich" Environment?

Stimulation is the main characteristic of a rich environment.

Stimulation is challenging.

Problem-solving (puzzles, discussions, word games) stimulates the brain.

Neurons grow when the brain works.

Part 4: The Brain and Memory

There are different types of memory, including linguistic memory and body learning.

We remember best in chunks, or groups of words.

Mnemonics are a good way to remember chunks.

Body memory, such as riding a bike, lasts a long time.

The brain and body remember together.

Part 5: Conclusion

This book is good for students and teachers.

Name: ______________________ Date: ______________

Graphic Organizer

Directions: Complete the graphic organizer below with information from the reading *The Joy of Work?*

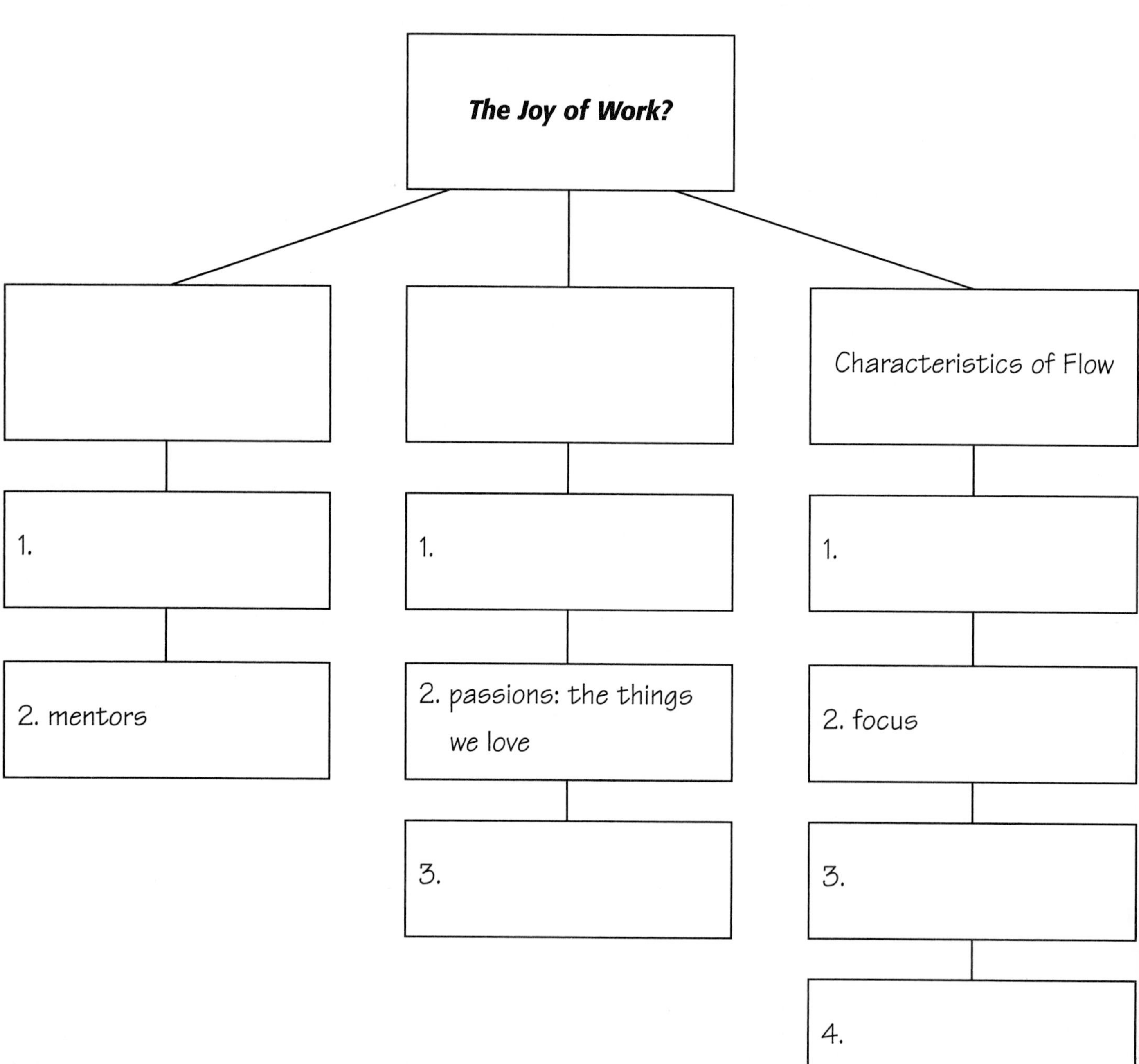

Name: ____ Date: ________________

Editing Practice

Directions: Find and correct the 10 mistakes in the paragraph below. The mistakes are with the future tense, gerunds, punctuation with the words *first, second, third,* and *however,* and the words for professions.

There are several things to think about if you are going be a language teacher. First you need to enjoy work with people. Second you should like the language and the people who speak the language. Third this profession involves work very hard. You may having a lot of students in your class. You might worked long hours preparing for classes. However you may find teacher very rewarding.

Name: ______________________ Date: ______________

Organizing Information

Directions: Complete the graphic organizer below with information from the reading *A Short History of Advertising.* Add circles as necessary.

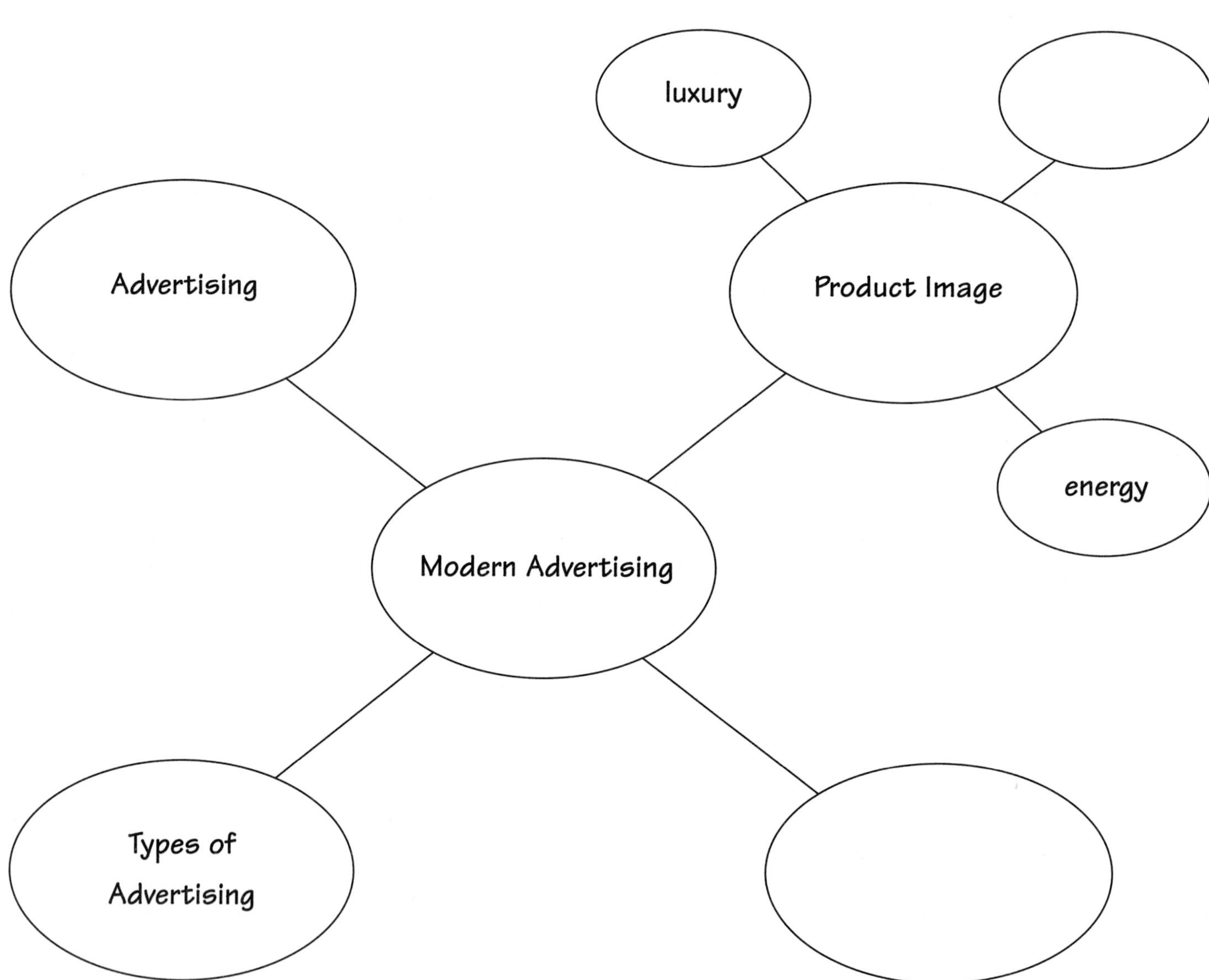

Match Up

1. Girls often play games that involve conversation, but	boys often use problem-solving in games.
2. Chimps need to get termites to eat, so	they use twigs as tools.
3. Female chimps spend more time with their mothers, so	they learn how to use the twigs faster.
4. Male chimps hunt to get meat, but	they don't always share.
5. Gender differences can be affected by our genes, or	they can be learned.
6. Toys can influence how much children talk, and	how active the children are.
7. Parents can't change their children's genes, but	they can affect what toys children use.
8. Some parents want to help daughters prepare for a career, so	they give them boys' toys.
9. Parents may want their boys to prepare for a career, but	they also want them to prepare for relationships.
10. Some stereotypes are negative, and	they negatively affect how well the targets do on certain tasks.
11. Positive stereotypes can be helpful, but	negative ones usually cause harm.
12. There are stereotypes about age, and	there are stereotypes about gender.

Name: ______________________________ **Date:** ______________

Editing Practice

Directions: Find and correct the eight mistakes in the paragraph below. The mistakes are in the use of *when, and, but, or, so, used to,* and punctuation.

When I was young my parents used to playing cards a lot. I didn't like cards and I liked to read. When my parents tried to get me to play cards with them, I use to refuse. I didn't like to waste my time. Now I have children. I enjoy playing games with them. Surprisingly, I even enjoy playing cards. I don't really like the card games but I like the conversations we have, when we play. There is sometimes more to a game than I thought. When parents and children play a game together they can have a stronger relationship.

Name: ______________________ Date: ______________

Crossword Puzzle

Directions: Complete the crossword below with words from Chapter 6.

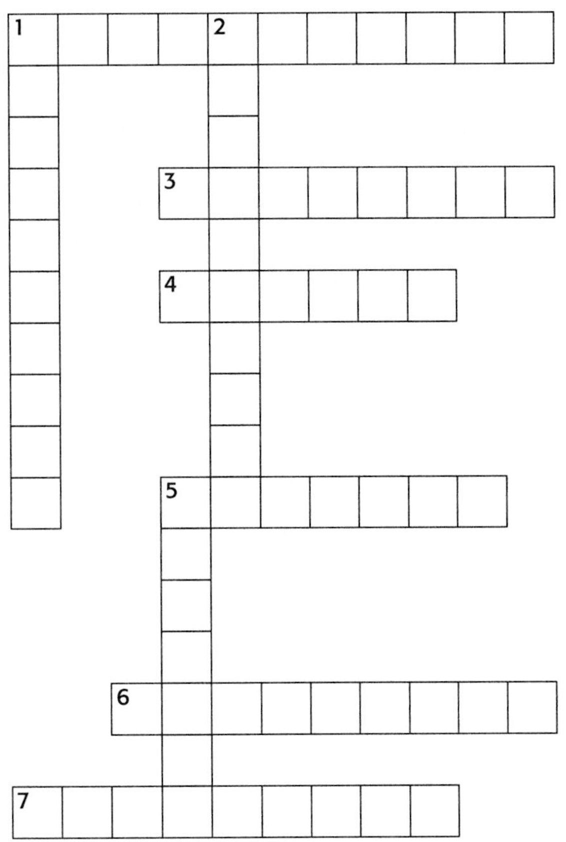

ACROSS
1. Be involved in
3. Army, navy, or other group that fights for a nation
4. One or the other
5. Beautiful and rich looking
6. Situation
7. Way of living

DOWN
1. The number of people living in a place
2. Person who is separate from a group
5. Learn about

Name:______________________________ **Date:**____________________ **Score:**________

❍ Reading Comprehension

Directions: Read the passage and sentences below. Fill in T if the sentence is *True* and F if the sentence is *False.*

Birth order seems to affect how children act and even the jobs they choose. The first child is often responsible and organized. First-born children usually follow rules and keep things in order. They are more likely to be scientists. The middle child usually gets along well with other people and is usually more relaxed. The middle child often chooses jobs where they work with people. The youngest child is often more creative and likes to have fun. While first-born children often choose intellectual careers—careers that use mental abilities—later-born children are more artistic and like to be outside. One reason for these differences could be that parents want the first child to do well and may worry more about them, but parents may be more relaxed with their younger children.

1. Birth order can influence personality and job choice. (T) (F)
2. Children who have older siblings are often creative. (T) (F)
3. Middle children are often friendly. (T) (F)
4. Parents don't worry about first-born children doing well. (T) (F)
5. Later-born children choose careers in science more than first-born children do. (T) (F)

❍ Strategy: Guessing the Meanings of New Words: Dashes

Directions: Fill in the bubble of the best meaning for the bold-faced word.

6. While first-born children often go into **intellectual careers**—careers that use mental abilities—later-born children are more artistic and like to be outside.

   (A) artistic jobs (C) mental jobs

   (B) creative jobs (D) outdoors jobs

7. If one identical twin is **outgoing**—the opposite of shy—the other twin is probably outgoing, too.

   (A) shy (C) tall

   (B) friendly (D) creative

8. **Fraternal** twins—non-identical twins—share about the same amount of genes as other siblings do.

   Ⓐ brother Ⓒ male
   Ⓑ not exactly alike Ⓓ exactly alike

9. Our **environment**—the place or conditions around us—can affect our personalities, too.

   Ⓐ personality Ⓒ education we receive
   Ⓑ genes Ⓓ situation around us

10. **Hereditary** traits—those that are inherited through a parent's DNA—often appear in several family members.

    Ⓐ physical Ⓒ received through genes
    Ⓑ nurturing Ⓓ identical

❍ Vocabulary

Directions: Complete each sentence with a word from the box.

designs	hero	identity	inherited	role
entertainment	identical	influenced	normal	share

11. In my favorite movie, the ______________________ saves a beautiful woman from danger.
12. When Brad's father died, he ______________________ his father's watch.
13. Ralph Lauren ______________________ clothing in the United States.
14. Young movie stars don't always have ______________________ childhoods because they are famous and earn a lot of money.
15. Mary and her sister wore ______________________ dresses to the party. They looked exactly the same.
16. My first grade teacher ______________________ me a lot. I wanted to be just like her.
17. I can't eat all of this cake. Do you want to ______________________it with me?
18. What do you do for ______________________ on the weekends?
19. Tom's ______________________ in the movie is small—he's the star's neighbor.
20. They didn't tell us the real ______________________ of the actor coming to visit because they didn't want a lot of people to come to the airport.

❍ Mechanics

Directions: Complete the paragraph with the correct form of each verb in parentheses.

My older sister Tina and I ____21____ (look) very different. We ____22____ (not act) alike either. During my childhood, she ____23____ (be) very important to me. I ____24____ (like) to follow her. She ____25____ (study) very hard. But I ____26____ (want) to have fun. Now she ____27____ (work) in a biology lab. I ____28____ (not do) anything scientific. I ____29____ (be) an artist. Yes, we ____30____ (be) different, but we love each other very much.

❍ Editing

Directions: Find and correct the five mistakes in tense, punctuation, and prepositions.

My aunt was a big influence of me now. She is interested in costume design. I am interested on design, too. I am similar from her in other ways. We both love movies and we both like to sing.

Name:________________ **Date:**________________ **Score:**________

❍ Reading Comprehension

Directions: Read the paragraph below and fill in the bubble of the correct answer for each comprehension question that follows.

Most college students have to remember a lot of information. This can be difficult. Students can become better at remembering information if they use memory strategies. One strategy is the use of mnemonic devices. Mnemonics are usually phrases, sentences, or songs that use the first letters of the words of things the student needs to remember. A problem with mnemonic devices is that they use memorizing skills and if the student has a bad memory, mnemonics may not help. Some people remember better if they draw pictures or make mental pictures that use the ideas they need to remember. Students can also improve their memories by using the strategy of trying to learn information a little at a time. Some people remember better if they say the information out loud. Other people remember better if they do something physical as they are learning the information they need to remember.

1. What is the main idea of the reading?

- Ⓐ Students can remember more if they use memory strategies.
- Ⓑ You can remember better if you draw pictures.
- Ⓒ Mnemonics are one way to remember information.

2. What is an example of a mnemonic?

- Ⓐ a mental picture
- Ⓑ saying something out loud
- Ⓒ a song that helps you remember something

3. Why don't mnemonics always work?

- Ⓐ you need to memorize the mnemonic
- Ⓑ you need to write it down
- Ⓒ you need to solve a problem

4. Why do college students need memory strategies?

- Ⓐ They can't remember very much.
- Ⓑ They have a lot to remember.
- Ⓒ They prefer to memorize, not think.

5. Which statement is true?

Ⓐ It's better to study for a long time, until you know all the material.

Ⓑ It's better to draw pictures than to say information aloud.

Ⓒ It's better to learn material a little at a time.

❍ Strategy: Understanding Tone

Directions: For each sentence below, identify the tone and fill in the correct bubble.

6. Hi, Mary. Meet me in the cafeteria after class.

Ⓐ Formal Ⓑ Informal

7. Dear Mr. Lee, I'm sorry I missed class today.

Ⓐ Formal Ⓑ Informal

8. I am writing to express my thanks for your invitation.

Ⓐ Formal Ⓑ Informal

9. Gotta run. See ya later.

Ⓐ Formal Ⓑ Informal

10. You're kidding!!!

Ⓐ Formal Ⓑ Informal

❍ Vocabulary

Directions: Complete each sentence with a word from the box.

active	challenging	mnemonic	passage	solution
approach	memorize	neuron	physically	stimulation

11. Maria read the ______________ three times, but she still didn't understand it.

12. We worked on the problem for a long time before we found a ______________.

13. In TPR, students listen to the teacher's commands and react ______________.

14. ______________ helps brain cells grow.

15. In the lexical ______________, students learn a lot of vocabulary by studying phrases.

16. Our teacher gives us 20 new words to ______________ each night.

17. A ______________ is a brain cell.

18. Some students remember words more easily if they use a ______________.

19. That class is very ______________—the students move around a lot.

20. I really enjoy ______________ problems because they make me think.

❍ Mechanics

Directions: Complete the paragraph below with *or, but,* or *because.*

I had a bad day yesterday. I couldn't find my English book ____________ (21) my dictionary. I left for class early, ____________ (22) I got lost and was late anyway. I think my teacher was upset with me ____________ (23) I was late on the first day of class. I didn't really meet my classmates ____________ (24) answer any questions ____________ (25) I'm too shy. There was one good thing that happened. During one activity, the teacher gave us a lot of commands, ____________ (26) we didn't have to say anything back. We just followed her directions. I really liked that part of class ____________ (27) I could respond physically and didn't have to talk. I know today wasn't perfect, ____________ (28) I think tomorrow will be better. I don't want to be late ____________ (29) lose my book again. I'm going to work hard in this class ____________ (30) I think English is important.

❍ Editing

Directions: Find and correct the five mistakes in punctuation, words after prepositions, and parts of speech (gerunds and simple forms of verbs).

It's a good idea to use a combination of methods to remembering things better, because different methods can help with different types of information. I really like use mnemonics for scientific information, but sometimes I forget mnemonics, too. Another way to remember is by make a mental picture. I really need to improving my memory because I'm studying a lot this semester.

Name:____________________ **Date:**_______________ **Score:**______

❍ Reading Comprehension

Directions: Read the paragraph below and fill in the bubble of the correct answer for each comprehension question that follows.

Are you just starting your career? Are you thinking about changing jobs? If so, you may want to follow certain steps. First, you should think about what you do well, or your skills, and tasks, or jobs, that you really enjoy. You can go online and take tests that will help you identify these talents and interests. You can also talk to a career counselor. After you list some jobs that might interest you, you can go online or to the library and do some research about what specific skills and education the jobs require. You might need to go back to school to get the education you need for some careers. Many people explore possible careers by getting an internship or volunteering. They often don't get paid, but they will find out a lot about the job.

1. What is the main idea of the reading?

- Ⓐ Many jobs require education and skills.
- Ⓑ You can go online to take tests and to research jobs.
- Ⓒ There are several ways people can find out what job they might want.

2. What is a task?

- Ⓐ a skill
- Ⓑ a job
- Ⓒ a test

3. What should you do first when you are looking into careers?

- Ⓐ think about your skills and what you enjoy
- Ⓑ talk to a counselor
- Ⓒ do some research

4. Which of the following is NOT a way to explore a career?

- Ⓐ volunteering
- Ⓑ getting an internship
- Ⓒ quitting a job

5. What is one way to find out what tasks you enjoy?

- Ⓐ take a test
- Ⓑ ask a counselor
- Ⓒ go to the library

❍ Strategy: Understanding Pronoun References

Directions: For each sentence below, fill in the bubble of the noun that the pronoun in bold refers to.

6. I really enjoy my new job. I get to meet lots of people. **It's** really exciting.

   Ⓐ I　Ⓑ my new job　Ⓒ lots of people

7. Both Harris and Seligman write about the discoveries of Mihaly Csikszentmihalyi. **He** studies a wonderful condition called "flow."

   Ⓐ Harris　Ⓑ Seligman　Ⓒ Csikszentmihalyi

8. Some psychologists suggest we identify our strengths and passions. Knowing **them** can help us to find happiness in work.

   Ⓐ psychologists　Ⓑ strengths and passions　Ⓒ workers

9. Teachers are often mentors to students. **They** can influence their students in many ways.

   Ⓐ teachers　Ⓑ mentors　Ⓒ students

10. The second reading had four paragraphs about different people and their careers. **They** were not difficult to understand.

   Ⓐ the four paragraphs　Ⓑ different people　Ⓒ careers

❍ Vocabulary

Directions: Complete each sentence with a word from the box.

admires	ancient	expert	passion	talent
advice	encouragement	gender	psychology	unfortunately

11. He enjoys studying ______________ people because he wants to understand how they lived long ago.

12. She ______________ her father for his many strengths.

13. I want to know why people think and act they way they do, so I'm studying ______________.

14. I'm not an ______________, but I do know a lot about the subject.

15. Lee's parents have always given him a lot of ______________. They tell him he can do anything if he tries.

16. I want to be a doctor. ______________, I'm not good at science.

17. In the United States, your ______________ doesn't matter for most jobs. Men and women apply for the same positions.

18. I have a ______________ for music. I love it more than anything else.

19. The counselor in that office gives career ______________.

20. She's really good at painting. She has a ______________ for it.

❍ Mechanics

Directions: Complete each sentence below with one of the words or phrases in parentheses.

21. I'm not sure what I want to do next summer. I ______________ (am going to/may) take a class.

22. She loves her class. ______________ (However/First), she doesn't like all the homework.

23. He is a ______________ (doctor/psychologist). He really enjoys medicine.

24. She wants to be a ______________ (tour guide/travel).

25. We ______________ (enjoy/involve) running, so we run together every day.

26. You can take psychology ______________ (or/but) archaeology at that time.

27. We ______________ (are going to/might) have a test tomorrow. The teacher told us it was certain.

28. Computer programming ______________ (enjoys/involves) working long hours on the computer.

29. First, list your talents and passions. ______________ (Second/However), do some research.

30. Linda's career is going to be in ______________ (education/teacher).

❍ Editing

Directions: Find and correct the five mistakes in punctuation, future tense, modals *(may/might)*, and words for professions.

Next year, I going to finish college. I don't know what kind of career I want. I may working as a teacher or I may do something in business. First, I want to travel. Second I need to move to a bigger city. I'm really interested in educating as a profession. However, I may discover that travel is really the profession for me.

Name:____________________ **Date:**________________ **Score:**________

❍ Reading Comprehension

Directions: Read the passage and sentences below. Fill in T if the sentence is *true* and F if the sentence is *false.*

Product placement is an effective way to advertise. It involves using real brand name products in scenes in movies, television shows, and video games. Product placement can make everyone happy if it is done well. The directors (and viewers) like it because the use of real products makes the situations more realistic. The advertisers like it because consumers get to see their products. Good product placement shows the product realistically, but doesn't make the product too obvious. Bad product placement makes the movie or TV show look like a really long commercial. Sometimes product placement just happens. The director decides a product will look good in a certain situation. Sometimes advertisers arrange for their products to be shown, in exchange for a certain amount of the product or for money.

1. The main idea of the reading is: Product placement just happens. (T) (F)

2. To use product placement effectively, you should make the product really obvious. (T) (F)

3. Advertisers sometimes pay to have their products shown on TV. (T) (F)

4. Product placement helps the advertiser, but not the moviemaker. (T) (F)

5. One problem with product placement is that making the product too obvious can make the movie or television show look like a commercial. (T) (F)

❍ Strategy: Recognizing Word Forms

Directions: For each word below, fill in the bubble to name the part of speech.

6. discoverer (A) verb (B) noun (C) adjective

7. entertainment (A) verb (B) noun (C) adjective

8. serious (A) verb (B) noun (C) adjective

9. advertise (A) verb (B) noun (C) adjective

10. environment (A) verb (B) noun (C) adjective

❍ Vocabulary

Directions: Complete each sentence with a word from the box.

attract	fans	improve	irritating	qualities
effective	image	incomes	personalize	specific

11. Advertisers try to create a product ______________, the values consumers connect with it.
12. They talk about the product's special ______________ or characteristics.
13. It's important to ______________ consumers who will buy the product.
14. The movie star has many ______________ who come to all his movies.
15. Advertisers get information about consumers through the Internet. This allows advertisers to ______________ the ads.
16. BMWs and other luxury cars appeal to people with higher ______________.
17. ______________ advertising gets customers to buy the product.
18. He was a really bad student last year, but hopefully this year he will ______________.
19. Some commercials are very ______________. They're too loud, and they say the same things again and again.
20. I couldn't find the ______________ shampoo I wanted, so I bought a different one.

❍ Mechanics

Directions: Complete each sentence below with one of the words or phrases in parentheses.

21. She ______________ (drives/is driving), so she can't talk on her cell phone.
22. (It's/There's) ______________ cold today.
23. (There's/There are) ______________ many people in the room.
24. He ______________ (goes/is going) to school every day.
25. They seem ______________ (nervous/nervously).
26. The teacher spoke ______________ (clear/clearly).

27. He gets in and starts the car. ________________ (First/After that), he checks the mirrors and puts his seat belt on.

28. She finished all her work at midnight. ________________ (At the beginning/Finally), she went to bed.

29. (There's/It's) ________________ a truck in the road.

30. The people ________________ (is standing/are standing) near the front of the store.

❍ Editing

Directions: Find and correct the five mistakes in subject-verb agreement, verb tense, adverbs, and commas with adverbs and with order words.

In this commercial, you see some people in a restaurant. It's a woman behind the counter. A customer is drinks coffee. Suddenly he spill his coffee. There is coffee all over the table. The woman gets a paper towel. Then she cleans up the coffee quick. The paper towel is very good for cleaning up.

Name:______________________________ **Date:**____________________ **Score:**________

❍ Reading Comprehension

Directions: Read the paragraph below and fill in the bubble of the correct answer for each comprehension question that follows.

In one study, researchers gave students two different tasks. One task involved dressing a doll, and the other task involved taking a toy apart and putting it back together. The students were put into three-person teams, and each student in a team had to complete one step of the task. Everyone on each team was of the same sex. Not surprisingly, the female teams were able to dress the doll more quickly, and the male teams were able to take the toy apart and put it together again more quickly. The results showed that students did better on the stereotypical tasks that matched their gender.

1. What is the main idea of the paragraph?
   - (A) Gender stereotypes affect how easily people complete tasks.
   - (B) People do better when they are on single-gender teams.
   - (C) Dressing dolls and taking toys apart are good practice for adulthood.
2. What type of stereotype were the researchers interested in?
   - (A) race
   - (B) gender
   - (C) age
3. What did each student have to do?
   - (A) complete one step of the task
   - (B) dress a doll
   - (C) work with three other people
4. What task was a stereotype of a girl's task?
   - (A) taking apart a toy
   - (B) putting a toy together
   - (C) dressing a doll
5. What does "not surprisingly" mean?
   - (A) It was a surprise.
   - (B) It wasn't a surprise.
   - (C) It wasn't what the researchers thought would happen.

❍ Strategy: Making Inferences

Directions: For each sentence below, fill in the bubble of the correct inference.

6. Stanford University accepted John because he got very good grades in high school.
   - (A) Stanford University accepts most students.
   - (B) You have to be a good student to go to Stanford.
   - (C) Stanford is similar to high school.

7. Every day, Mary and her sister play with toy trucks instead of dolls.
   - (A) Mary likes "girl toys."
   - (B) Mary's parents let their daughters play with "boy toys."
   - (C) Mary wants to be a truck driver.

8. Meat is a necessary source of protein. Male chimpanzees don't often share meat with female chimpanzees, so termites are important food for the females.
   - (A) Termites are a source of protein.
   - (B) Female chimpanzees share more than male chimpanzees.
   - (C) Meat is better than termites as a source of protein.

9. Toys help prepare children for adulthood.
   - (A) Adults play as much as children.
   - (B) Children become adults when they play.
   - (C) Children practice to be adults through play.

10. Not surprisingly, the female teams were able to dress the doll more quickly, and the male teams were able to take the toy apart and reassemble it more quickly.
    - (A) Females are better at dressing.
    - (B) Putting toys together is a stereotype of a boy's task.
    - (C) Boys are faster than girls.

❍ Vocabulary

Directions: Fill in the bubble for the word or phrase that best completes each sentence.

11. A ________________ studies social groups and society.

(A) researcher (B) psychologist (C) sociologist

12. When I need to relax, I ________________ I'm at the beach.

(A) imagine (B) prepare (C) take apart

13. When you reach ________________, you can do things you couldn't do as a child.

(A) fatherhood (B) childhood (C) adulthood

14. Girls are often more ________________ than boys.

(A) vocal (B) general (C) elderly

15. The ________________ show that stereotypes can be both good and bad.

(A) choices (B) targets (C) results

16. There were too many ________________. I couldn't decide what I wanted.

(A) races (B) tasks (C) choices

17. She has a good ____________ with her daughter.

Ⓐ relationship Ⓑ adulthood Ⓒ result

18. When I was an ____________, my mother held me all the time.

Ⓐ adult Ⓑ infant Ⓒ elderly

19. John is shy, so he's not very good at ____________.

Ⓐ eye contact Ⓑ research Ⓒ questionnaires

20. I enjoy solving problems. I like to ____________ and then put them back together.

Ⓐ prepare things Ⓑ take things apart Ⓒ fill things out

❍ Mechanics

Directions: Complete the paragraph below with *when, so, or, and,* or *but.*

____(21)____ I was young, I used to play with my sisters. We didn't have a lot of money, ____(22)____ we didn't buy many toys. We used to imagine we were at the grocery store, ____(23)____ we bought lots of food. Sometimes we played with dolls, ____(24)____ I didn't like that very much. I liked it ____(25)____ we "traveled" to other places. My sister Anna didn't always play with us. She liked to read a book ____(26)____ watch TV. My sister Tina was the oldest, ____(27)____ she usually was the responsible one. Tina ____(28)____ Anna used to get mad at me sometimes. I didn't listen very well ____(29)____ help clean up, ____(30)____ I did have a lot of fun.

❍ Editing

Directions: Find and correct the five mistakes in punctuation, conjunctions, and the phrase *used to.*

When John was a little boy he use to live in a city. There were many cars on the street, but it wasn't a safe place to play. He used stay inside his apartment and watch TV all the time. Now, John is an adult and he is very active. No more TV for him.

Name:________________ **Date:**____________ **Score:**______

❍ Reading Comprehension

Directions: Read the passage and sentences below. Fill in T if the sentence is *true* and F if the sentence is *false*.

The Aruntas are a tribe in Australia. They have a coming-of-age ceremony for boys who are about 12 years old. When a boy is about 12 years old, he must leave the women and girls and go to a men's camp. The mother of the boy's future wife gives the boy a burning stick. The boy must keep the fire going to symbolize his undying love for his future wife. The men paint the boy's body with designs. Older men dance and tell stories. For three days, the men teach the boy the things he must know to be a man in their culture. Finally, he can rejoin the rest of the tribe.

1. The main idea of this passage is: Boys in the Arunta tribe must keep a stick burning. Ⓣ Ⓕ
2. The boy is separated from the females for three days. Ⓣ Ⓕ
3. A burning stick symbolizes the boy's passage into adulthood. Ⓣ Ⓕ
4. The boy is alone for most of the ceremony. Ⓣ Ⓕ
5. This ritual follows the three stages of separation, transition, and incorporation. Ⓣ Ⓕ

❍ Strategy: Finding Details

Directions: Choose the best answer. Fill in the bubble.

6. "In my family, we practice many rituals that bring us closer together." For this main idea, what would be a good detail sentence?
   - Ⓐ We eat together as a family almost every night.
   - Ⓑ My father's name is Frank.
   - Ⓒ My family likes to eat many different types of food.

7. "My friends love spending time with my family." For this main idea, what would be a good detail sentence?
   - (A) I have three brothers and sisters.
   - (B) For one thing, there's always plenty of food.
   - (C) Henry is one of my friends.
8. "Everyone gives the birthday boy or girl a present." This would be a good detail for which main idea?
   - (A) My birthday is in March.
   - (B) You can go shopping early.
   - (C) Birthdays and holidays are special in my family.
9. "We play games together, or sometimes rent a movie." This would be a good detail for which main idea?
   - (A) One night a week is "family night."
   - (B) I like to play chess.
   - (C) We eat at the same time every night.
10. The three sentences below could be written as one paragraph. Which sentence is the main idea?
    - (A) You need to wear a special costume.
    - (B) You hold a candle and sing a traditional song.
    - (C) You must go through an initiation ceremony to join that club.

❍ Vocabulary

Directions: Complete each sentence with a word from the box.

club	elegant	rejoined	strict	transition
dating	escort	rituals	symbolizes	tuxedo

11. Many cultures have ________________ that mark the passage from childhood to adulthood.
12. It was a very formal dance, so Petra wore an ________________ dress.
13. Petra's boyfriend Marco was her ________________ to the dance.
14. Marco wore a ________________.
15. The Amish have many rules. It is a very ________________ society.
16. My parents don't think ________________ is a good idea until I am at least 16.
17. Teenagers experience many changes. The teenage years are a period of ________________.

18. Tomas went out alone for a while, but he ______________ the group later.

19. In China, the color red ______________ good fortune, or luck.

20. I wanted to belong to a ______________, so I joined one in high school.

❍ Mechanics

Directions: Complete the paragraph with one of the words or phrases in parentheses.

Getting a driver's license in the United States is like a rite ______(21)______ (of/on) passage. In most states, you ______(22)______ (have to/have) be 16 years of age, ______(23)______ (and/but) you must ______(24)______ (take/to take) a driver's education class. There are two parts. ______(25)______ (First/Second), you learn rules of the road in the classroom. ______(26)______ (Next/At the end), you take a driving class. You learn many things, including how to turn ______(27)______ (on/in) the headlights, and put ______(28)______ (on/off) the flashing lights to indicate a problem. ______(29)______ (After that/After a while), you ______(30)______ (have to/have) pass a written test to get a learner's permit. After you practice some more, you can take a test to get your license.

❍ Editing

Directions: Find and correct the five mistakes in punctuation, subject-verb agreement, and *must* + the simple form of the verb.

When boys in the Jewish religion are 13 years old they can celebrate a coming-of-age ceremony known as a *bar mitzvah.* The boy must studies for a long time. On the day of the bar mitzvah, the boy must reciting a passage and chant some prayers in a religious ceremony. After that there is a big party. His friends and family usually brings him gifts.

Chapter 1

Reading Comprehension

1. T; 2. T; 3. T; 4. F; 5. F

Strategy: Guessing the Meanings of New Words: Dashes

6. C; 7. B; 8. B; 9. D; 10. C

Vocabulary

11. hero; 12. inherited; 13. designs; 14. normal; 15. identical; 16. influenced; 17. share; 18. entertainment; 19. role; 20. identity

Mechanics

21. look; 22. don't act; 23. was; 24. liked; 25. studied; 26. wanted; 27. works; 28. don't do; 29. am; 30. are

Editing

My aunt ~~was~~ [is] a big influence ~~of~~ [on] me now. She is interested in costume design. I am interested ~~on~~ [in] design, too. I am similar ~~from~~ [to] her in other ways. We both love movies[,] and we both like to sing.

Chapter 2

Reading Comprehension

1. A; 2. C; 3. A; 4. B; 5. C

Strategy: Understanding Tone

6. B; 7. A; 8. A; 9. B; 10. B

Vocabulary

11. passage; 12. solution; 13. physically; 14. Stimulation; 15. approach; 16. memorize; 17. neuron; 18. mnemonic; 19. active; 20. challenging

Mechanics

21. or; 22. but; 23. because; 24. or; 25. because; 26. but; 27. because; 28. but; 29. or; 30. because

Editing

It's a good idea to use a combination of methods to remember~~ing~~ things better/ because different methods can help with different types of information. I really like us~~e~~ [ing] mnemonics for scientific information, but sometimes I forget mnemonics, too. Another way to remember is by mak~~e~~ [ing] a mental picture. I really need to improv~~ing~~ [e] my memory because I'm studying a lot this semester.

Chapter 3

Reading Comprehension

1. C; 2. B; 3. A; 4. C; 5. A

Strategy: Understanding Pronoun References

6. B; 7. C; 8. B; 9. A; 10. A

Vocabulary

11. ancient; 12. admires; 13. psychology; 14. expert; 15. encouragement; 16. Unfortunately; 17. gender; 18. passion; 19. advice; 20. talent

Mechanics

21. may; 22. However; 23. doctor; 24. tour guide; 25. enjoy; 26. or; 27. are going to; 28. involves; 29. Second; 30. education

Editing

Next year, I [am] going to finish college. I don't know what kind of career I want. I may work~~ing~~ as a teacher[,] or I may do something in business. First, I want to travel. Second[,] I need to move to a bigger city. I'm really interested in educat~~ing~~ [ion] as a profession. However, I may discover that travel is really the profession for me.

Chapter 4

Reading Comprehension

1. F; 2. F; 3. T; 4. F; 5. T

Strategy: Recognizing Word Forms

6. B; 7. B; 8. C; 9. A; 10. B

Vocabulary

11. image; 12. qualities; 13. attract; 14. fans; 15. personalize; 16. incomes; 17. Effective; 18. improve; 19. irritating; 20. specific

Mechanics

21. is driving; 22. It's; 23. There are; 24. goes; 25. nervous; 26. clearly; 27. After that; 28. Finally; 29. There's; 30. are standing

Editing

In this commercial, you see some people in a restaurant. ~~It's~~ There's a woman behind the counter. A customer is drink~~s~~ing coffee. Suddenly, he spills his coffee. There is coffee all over the table. The woman gets a paper towel. Then she cleans up the coffee quickly. The paper towel is very good for cleaning up.

Chapter 5

Reading Comprehension

1. A; 2. B; 3. A; 4. C; 5. B

Strategy: Making Inferences

6. B; 7. B; 8. A; 9. C; 10. B

Vocabulary

11. C; 12. A; 13. C; 14. A; 15. C; 16. C; 17. A; 18. B; 19. A; 20. B

Mechanics

21. When; 22. so; 23. and; 24. but; 25. when; 26. or; 27. so; 28. and; 29. or; 30. but

Editing

When John was a little boy, he used to live in a city. There were many cars on the street, ~~but~~ so it wasn't a safe place to play. He used to stay inside his apartment and watch TV all the time. Now, John is an adult, and he is very active. No more TV for him.

Chapter 6

Reading Comprehension

1. F; 2. T; 3. F; 4. F; 5. T

Strategy: Finding Details

6. A; 7. B; 8. C; 9. A; 10. C

Vocabulary

11. rituals; 12. elegant; 13. escort; 14. tuxedo; 15. strict; 16. dating; 17. transition; 18. rejoined; 19. symbolizes; 20. club

Mechanics

21. of; 22. have to; 23. and; 24. take; 25. First; 26. Next; 27. on; 28. on; 29. After that; 30. have to

Editing

When boys in the Jewish religion are 13 years old, they can celebrate a coming-of-age ceremony known as a *bar mitzvah*. The boy must stud~~ies~~y for a long time. On the day of the bar mitzvah, the boy must recit~~ing~~e a passage and chant some prayers in a religious ceremony. After that, there is a big party. His friends and family usually bring~~s~~ him gifts.